BEST-EVER
SALADS

~

BEST-EVER SALADS

THE DEFINITIVE
COOK'S COLLECTION:
200 MOUTHWATERING RECIPES

CONSULTING EDITOR:
STEVEN WHEELER

HERMES
HOUSE

This edition published by Hermes House
27 West 20th Street, New York, NY 10011

HERMES HOUSE books are available for bulk purchase for sales promotion
and for premium use. For details, write or call the sales director,
Hermes House, 27 West 20th Street, New York, NY 10011

Hermes House is an imprint of Anness Publishing Inc.

ISBN 1 84309 166 6

Publisher: Joanna Lorenz
Senior Editor: Joanne Rippin
Designer: Bill Mason
Illustrator: Anna Koska
Editorial Reader: Richard McGinlay

Printed and bound in Hong Kong

CONTENTS

INTRODUCTION

~

Introduction

A well-made salad is almost lyrical in its combination of fresh tastes, textures and colors expressing a particular mood or theme. This book looks at a variety of salad themes and shows that there is more to salads than meets the eye.

Seasonal changes are important and provide a useful lead when you are searching for inspiration. The finest salads begin with one or two ingredients that serve as a focal point. If you come across a perfect pear, partner it with a handful of toasted pecans and a few leaves of young spinach and drizzle on a blue cheese dressing. If a freshly boiled crab sounds appealing, consider the strong flavors of avocado, cilantro and lime. Some new potatoes and young lettuce leaves will make it a salad to remember.

Most salads fit into the summer season and are inspired by an abundance of freshness and color. Summer salads are best eaten outside. In autumn and winter we move inside to enjoy such treats as wild mushrooms, duck and chicken livers. The richness of these ingredients combines especially well with hearty oat leaf lettuce, escarole and chicory. Spring sees the arrival of young vegetables and tender salad leaves such as spinach and arugula. These delicate flavors go well with simply-grilled fish, eggs, ham and chicken. In fact, simplicity is the key to a successful salad: when two or more ingredients are combined, their flavors should work well together but still be identifiable.

Whether you want a snack or a full meal, a side dish or a celebratory feast, this book has a salad for every occasion. There are cooked and uncooked salads using a vast range of vegetables, pasta, rice, fish, meat, poultry and fruit, all of them mouth-wateringly good.

May your salads bring good health and happiness to your table!

Salad Vegetables

A salad vegetable is any type of vegetable that earns its keep in a salad by virtue of freshness and flavor. Vegetables for a salad can be raw or lightly cooked. If cooked, they are best served at room temperature to bring out their full flavor. Here is a selection of the most commonly used salad vegetables.

Avocado

This has a smooth, buttery flesh when ripe and is an asset to many salads, of which Guacamole is perhaps the best known. Avocados can also be served on their own as an appetizer, with a light vinaigrette or a spoonful of lemony mayonnaise, or even just a squeeze of lemon juice and salt.

Baby Corn

Baby corn cobs can be eaten whole, lightly cooked or raw, and should be served warm or at room temperature.

Carrots

These should be young and sweet. Either cooked or raw, they bring flavor and color to a salad.

Celery

A useful salad vegetable, celery is grown year round for its robust, earthy flavor. The crisp stems should be neither stringy nor tough. Celery partners well with ham, apples and walnuts in Waldorf Salad and is also used as a crudité.

Cucumbers

A common salad ingredient that turns up in salad bowls everywhere. The quality of this vegetable is best appreciated in strongly–flavored salads.

Fennel

The bulb (or Florence) variety has a strong, aniseed flavor and looks like a squat head of celery. Because the flavor can be dominant, it may be blanched in boiling water for 6 minutes before being used in a salad.

Garlic

Strong to taste, garlic is essential to the robust cooking of South America, Asia and the Mediterranean. Garlic should be used carefully, as it can mask other flavors, but it is a vital part of salad preparation. To impart a very gentle hint of garlic, rub around the inside of your salad bowl with a cut clove. Another way to moderate the strength of fresh garlic is to store a few crushed cloves in a bottle of olive oil, and use the oil sparingly in dressings.

Green beans

The varieties are too numerous to mention here, but they all have their merits as salad vegetables. To appreciate the sweet flavor of young tender green beans, cook them for 6 minutes and then refresh immediately in cold running water so that the crispness and color are retained. An essential ingredient of Salade Niçoise, green beans are an ideal crudité and also partner well with a spicy tomato sauce.

Mushrooms

These provide richness to many salads and are eaten both raw and cooked. The oyster mushroom, which grows wild but is also cultivated, has a fine flavor and texture. White mushrooms are widely available and are often used raw, thinly sliced, in salads. Chestnut mushrooms are similar to white mushrooms but have slightly more flavor.

Onions

Several varieties are suited to salads. The strongest is the small, yellow onion, which should be chopped finely and used sparingly. Less strong is the large, white Spanish onion, which has a sweeter, milder flavor and may be used coarsely chopped.

Potatoes

A staple carbohydrate ingredient to add bulk to a salad or provide a main element.

Scallions

These have a milder flavor than the common onion and give a gentle bite to many popular salads.

Tomatoes

Technically a fruit rather than a vegetable, tomatoes are valued for their flavor and color. Dwarf varieties usually ripen more quickly than large ones and have a better flavor.

Zucchini

These can be bitter and are usually cooked before being combined with other vegetables. Smooth in texture when cooked, they go well with tomatoes, eggplant, bell peppers and onions. Use baby zucchini for a sweeter flavor if you want to serve raw zucchini as a crudité.

Salad Fruits

The contents of the fruit bowl offer endless possibilities for sweet and savory salads.

Apples
This versatile fruit offers a unique flavor to both sweet and savory salads.

Apricots
Use apricots raw or lightly poached.

Bananas
These bring a special richness to fruit salads, although their flavor can often interfere with more delicate fruit.

Blackberries
With a very short season, wild blackberries have more flavor than cultivated ones.

Blueberries
These tight-skinned berries combine well with the sharpness of fresh oranges.

Cape Gooseberries
Small, fragrant, pleasantly tart orange berries, wrapped in a paper "cape."

Cherries
Cherries should be firm and glossy and are a delicious and colorful ingredient in many kinds of salad.

Cranberries
Too sharp to eat raw but very good for cooking.

Dates
Fresh dates are sweet and juicy, dried ones have a more intense flavor. Both kinds work well in fresh fruit salads.

Figs
Green or purple skinned fruit, with sweet, pinkish-red flesh. Eat whole or peeled.

Gooseberries
Dessert types can be eaten raw but cooking varieties are more widely available.

Grapefruit
These can have yellow, green or pink flesh; the pink-fleshed or ruby varieties are the sweetest.

Grapes
Large Muscat varieties, whose season runs from late summer to autumn, are the most coveted and also the most expensive.

Kiwi
Available all year round.

Kumquats
Tiny relatives of the orange and can be eaten raw or cooked.

Lemons and limes
Both of these citrus fruits are used for flavor and to prevent fruit from turning brown.

Lychees
A small fruit with a hard pink skin and sweet, juicy flesh.

Mangoes
Tropical fruit with an exotic flavor and golden-orange flesh that is wonderful in sweet or savory salads.

Melons
These grow in abundance from mid-to late summer and provide freshness and flavor. Melon is at its most delicious served ice cold.

Nectarines
A relative of the peach with a smoother skin.

Oranges
At their best during winter, they can be segmented and added to sweet and savory salads.

Papayas
These fruits of the tropics have a distinctive, sweet flavor. When ripe they are yellow–green.

Peaches
Choose white peaches for the sweetest flavor and yellow for a stronger taste.

Pears
Perfect for savory salads and with strong blue cheese and toasted pecans.

Pineapples
Ripe pineapples resist firm pressure in the hand and have a sweet smell.

Plums
There are many dessert and cooking varieties.

Raspberries
Much coveted berries that partner well with ripe mango, passion fruit and strawberries.

Rhubarb
Technically a vegetable, too tart to eat raw.

Star fruit
When sliced, this makes a pretty shape perfect for garnishes.

Strawberries
A popular summer fruit, sometimes served with cream.

Lettuces and Leaves

One particular aspect of lettuce that sets it apart from any other vegetable is that you can only buy it in one form—fresh.

Lettuce has been cultivated for thousands of years. In Egyptian times it was sacred to the fertility god Min. It was then considered a powerful aphrodisiac, yet for the Greeks and the Romans it was thought to have quite the opposite effect, making one sleepy and generally soporific. Chemists today confirm that lettuce contains a hypnotic similar to opium, and in herbal remedies lettuce is recommended for insomniacs.

There are hundreds of different varieties of lettuce. Today, an increasing choice is available, so the salad bowl can become a wealth of color, taste and texture with no other ingredient than a selection of leaves.

Boston

These are the classic round lettuces seen in kitchen gardens. They have a pale heart and floppy, loosely packed leaves. They have a pleasant flavor as long as they are fresh. Choose the lettuce with the best heart by picking it up at the bottom and gently squeezing to check that there is a firm center.

Lollo Rosso

Lollo rosso and lollo biondo—similar in shape but a paler green without any purple edges—are both non-hearting lettuces. Although they do not have a lot of flavor, they look superb and are often used as garnishes or to form a nest of leaves on which to place the main ingredients of a salad.

Romaine

Romaine is the only lettuce that would have been known in antiquity. It has two names, Romaine, used in the United States and France, derived from the Greek island where it was found by the Romans. Cos is considered to have the best flavor and is the correct lettuce for use in Caesar Salad.

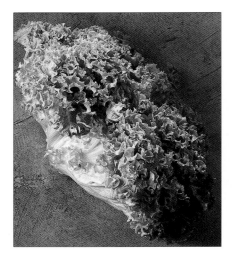

Escarole

Escarole is one of the more robust lettuces in terms of flavor and texture. Like the curly-leafed endive, escarole has a distinct bitter flavor. Served with other leaves and a well-flavored dressing to temper the bitterness, escarole and endive will give your salad a pleasant "bite."

Oak Leaf Lettuce

Oak leaf lettuce, together with lollo rosso and lollo biondo, is another member of the loosehead lettuce group. Oak leaf lettuce has a very gentle flavor and will need a dressing of the highest quality ingredients. It is a very decorative leaf and makes a beautiful addition to any salad and a lovely garnish.

Little Gem
In appearance little gems look like something between a baby Romaine and a tightly-furled Boston. They have firm hearts and a distinct flavor. Their tight centers mean that they can be sliced while still whole and the quarters used for holding slivers of smoked fish or anchovies as a simple appetizer.

Chinese Cabbage
Chinese cabbage has pale green, crinkly leaves with long, wide, white ribs. Its shape is a little like a very fat head of celery, which gives rise to another of its names, celery cabbage. It is pleasantly crunchy and, since it is available year round, it makes a useful winter salad component.

Radicchio
This is one of the many varieties developed from wild chicory. It looks like a lettuce with deep wine-red leaves and striking cream ribs and owes its splendid foliage to careful shading from the light. If it is grown in the dark the leaves are marbled pink. Its bitter flavor contrasts well with green salads.

Mache
Mache or lamb's lettuce is a popular winter leaf that does not actually belong to the lettuce family, but it makes a lovely addition to salads. Called lamb's lettuce in England, mache has small, attractive, dark green leaves and grows in pretty little sprigs. Its flavor is mild and nutty.

Watercress
Watercress is perhaps the most robustly flavored of all the salad ingredients, and a handful of watercress is all you need to perk up an otherwise dull salad. It has a distinctive raw flavor, both peppery and slightly pungent, and this, together with its bright green leaves, makes it a popular garnish.

Arugula
Arugula has a wonderful peppery flavor and is excellent in a mixed green salad. It was eaten by the Greeks and Romans as an aphrodisiac. Since it has such a striking flavor, a little goes a long way, and just a few leaves will transform a green salad and liven up a sandwich.

Herbs

For as long as salads draw on the qualities of fresh produce, sweet herbs will have an important part to play in providing individual character and flavor. When herbs are used in a salad, they should be as full of life as the salad leaves they accompany. Dried herbs are no substitute for fresh ones and should be reserved for cooked dishes such as casseroles. Salad herbs are distinguished by their ability to release flavor without lengthy cooking.

Most salad herbs belong finely chopped in salad dressings and marinades, while the robust flavors of rosemary, thyme and fennel branches can be used on the barbecue to impart a smoky herb flavor. Ideally, salad herbs should be picked just before use, but if you cannot use them immediately keep their stems in water to retain their freshness. Parsley, mint and cilantro will keep for up to a week in this way if also covered with a plastic bag and placed in the refrigerator.

Basil
Remarkable for its fresh, pungent flavor unlike that of any other herb, basil is widely used in Mediterranean salads, especially Italian recipes. Basil leaves are tender and delicate and should be gently torn or snipped with scissors, rather than chopped with a knife.

Chives
Chives belong to the onion family and have a mild onion flavor. The slender, green stems and soft mauve flowers are both edible. Chives are an indispensable flavoring for potato salads.

Cilantro
The chopped leaves of this pungent, distinctively flavored herb are popular in Middle Eastern and Asian salads.

Lavender
This soothingly fragrant herb is edible and may be used in both sweet and savory salads, as it goes well with thyme, garlic, honey and orange.

Mint
This much-loved herb is widely used in Greek and Middle Eastern salads, such as Tzatziki and Tabbouleh. It is also a popular addition to fruit salads. Garden mint is the most common variety; others include spearmint and the round-leafed apple mint.

Above: Clockwise from top left; thyme, cilantro, parsley, chives, lavender, rose, mint and basil.

Parsley
Flat- and curly-leaf parsley are both used for their fresh, green flavor. Flat-leaf parsley is said to have a stronger taste. Freshly chopped parsley is used by the handful in salads and dressings.

Rose
Although it is not technically an herb, the sweet-scented rose can be used to flavor fresh fruit salads. It combines well with blackberries and raspberries.

Thyme
An asset to salads featuring rich, earthy flavors, this herb has a penetrating flavor.

Spices

Spices are the aromatic seasonings found in the seed, bark, fruit and sometimes flowers of certain plants and trees. The value of spices has been appreciated in Europe since the Arabs first monopolized the Eastern spice trade over 3,000 years ago. Prices remained high until ocean trade was established by Britain in the seventeenth century. Today we still value spices for their warm, inviting flavors, and thankfully their price is relatively low. The flavor of a spice is contained in the volatile oils of the seed, bark or fruit; so, like herbs, spices should be used as fresh as possible. Whole spices keep better than ground ones, which tend to lose their freshness in 3–4 months.

Not all spices are suitable for salad making, although many allow us to explore the flavors of other cultures. The recipes in this book use curry spices in moderation so as not to spoil the delicate salad flavors. The moderate use of Indian spices is found in French cooking, where spices are employed with respect for underlying flavor.

Above: Flavorful additions to salads include (clockwise from top left) celery salt, caraway seeds, curry paste, saffron strands, peppercorns and cayenne pepper.

Caraway

These savory-sweet tasting seeds are widely used in German and Austrian cooking and feature strongly in many Jewish dishes. The small ribbed seeds are similar in appearance and taste to cumin. The flavor combines especially well with German mustard in a dressing for a variety of salads.

Cayenne pepper

Also known as chili powder, this is the dried and finely ground fruit of the hot chile pepper. It is an important seasoning in South American cooking and is often used when seasoning fish and seafood. Cayenne pepper can be blended with paprika if it is too hot and should be used with care, as a little goes a long way.

Celery salt

A combination of ground celery seed and salt, this is used for seasoning vegetables, especially carrots.

Curry paste

Prepared curry paste consists of a blend of Indian spices preserved in oil. It may be added to dressings, and is particularly useful in this respect for showing off the sweet qualities of fish and shellfish.

Pepper

The most popular spice used in the West, pepper features in the cooking of almost every nation. Peppercorns can be white, black, green or red and should always be freshly milled rather than bought already ground.

Saffron

The world's most expensive spice, made from the dried stigma of a crocus, real saffron has a tobacco-rich smell and gives a sweet yellow tint to liquids used for cooking. It can be used in creamy dressings and brings out the richness of fish and seafood dishes. There are many powdered imitations that provide color without the flavor of the real thing.

Oils, Vinegars and Flavorings

OILS

Oil is the main ingredient of most dressings and provides an important richness to salads. Neutral oils, such as sunflower, safflower or peanut, are ideally used as a background for stronger oils. Sesame, walnut and hazelnut oils are the strongest and should be used sparingly. Olive oil is prized for its clarity of flavor and healthfulness. The most significant producers of olive oil are Italy, France, Spain and Greece. These and other countries produce two main grades of olive oil: estate-grown extra-virgin olive oil, for which olives have been mechanically picked and often warmed before pressing to extract a higher percentage of oil, and semi-fine olive oil, of an ordinary standard.

Olive oils

French olive oils are subtly flavored and provide a well-balanced lightness to dressings. The golden oil featured here has a sweet, fruity flavor and is suited to the foods of southern France.

Greek olive oils are typically strong in character. They are often green with a thick texture and are unsuitable for mayonnaise.

Italian olive oils are noted for their vigorous Mediterranean flavors and suggest grassy herbs—often a prickly taste of black pepper. Tuscan oils are noted for their well-rounded, spicy flavor and are often green in color. Sicilian oils tend to be lighter in texture, although they are often more strongly flavored than Tuscan oils.

Spanish olive oils are typically fruity and often have a nutty quality with a pleasant bitterness.

Nut oils

Hazelnut and walnut oils are valued for their strong, nutty flavor. Tasting richly of the nuts from which they are pressed, both are usually blended with neutral oils for salad dressings.

Seed oils

Peanut and sunflower oils are valued by many cooks for their clean, neutral flavor.

SALAD FLAVORINGS

Capers

Capers are the pickled flower buds of a bush native to the Mediterranean. Their strong, sharp flavor is well suited to richly flavored salads. Smaller, tightly packed capers are more intensely flavored than larger varieties.

Lemon and lime juice

The juice of lemons and limes is used to impart a clean acidity to oil dressings. Both have a similar strength to vinegar and should be used in moderation.

Mustard

Mustard has a tendency to bring out the flavor of other ingredients. It acts as an emulsifier in dressings and allows oil and vinegar to merge for a short period of time. Whenever possible, French, German and English mustards should be used for salads of the same nationality.

Olives

Black and green olives belong in salads with a Mediterranean flavor. Black olives are generally sweeter than green ones, although many green olives are treated with sugar and sometimes lemon juice to bring out their flavor.

VINEGARS

White wine vinegar is probably the most popular type for salad dressings, but it should be used in moderation to balance the richness of an oil. There are many other vinegars from which to choose; however, a good-quality white wine vinegar will serve most purposes.

Making Herbal Oils and Vinegars

Many herbal oils and vinegars are available commercially, but you can very easily make your own. Pour the oil or vinegar into a jar and add your flavoring. Let steep for 2 weeks, then strain and decant into an attractive bottle. Add a seal and an identifying label.

Here are some ideas for flavored oils and vinegars.

Left: Top left to right; Italian virgin olive oil, Spanish olive oil, Italian olive oil, Safflower oil, hazelnut oil, walnut oil, peanut oil, French olive oil, Italian olive oil, white wine vinegar. Left to right bottom; lemon, olives, limes, capers and mustard.

When using fresh herbs to flavor oil or vinegar, make sure they are clean and completely dry before you use them.

BASIL AND CHILI OIL

Steep basil and 3 chiles in virgin olive oil, then decant. Put 2 sprigs of basil and 3 chiles in the bottle to decorate. Add to tomato and mozzarella salads.

DILL AND LEMON OIL

Steep a handful of fresh dill and a large strip of lemon zest in virgin olive oil, then decant. Add 2 large fronds of dill and 2 strips of lemon peel to the bottle. Use for salads containing fish or seafood.

MEDITERRANEAN HERB OIL

Steep rosemary, thyme and marjoram in virgin olive oil, then decant. Decorate with herbs tied around a cinnamon stick.

MIXED HERB OIL

Steep sage, rosemary, tarragon and marjoram in virgin olive oil, then decant. Bind a selection of the herbs with string and add to the bottle.

MIXED HERB VINEGAR

Steep sage, thyme, bay and marjoram in white wine vinegar, then decant. Tie a selection of the herbs into a bunch and wind around with string. Insert into the bottle.

ROSEMARY AND RED WINE VINEGAR

Steep a sprig of fresh rosemary in red wine vinegar, then decant and add a few long stems of rosemary plus some pink rose petals.

TARRAGON VINEGAR

Steep tarragon in cider vinegar, then decant. Insert 2 or 3 long sprigs of tarragon into the bottle.

THYME OIL

Steep a handful of thyme in virgin olive oil, then decant. Add 2 large sprigs of thyme to the bottle for decoration and identification.

Left: Beautiful and delicious, herbal oils make exquisite gifts. From left to right: basil and chili; Mediterranean herb; dill and lemon; thyme; and mixed herb.

Vegetable Preparation

SHREDDING CABBAGE

Cabbage features in many salad recipes, such as coleslaw, and this method for shredding can be used for white, green or red varieties.

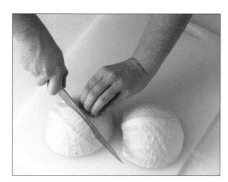

1 Use a large knife to cut the cabbage into quarters.

2 Cut the hard core from each quarter and discard; this part is not really edible when raw.

3 Slice each quarter to form fine shreds. Shredded cabbage will keep for several hours in the fridge, but do not dress it until you are ready to serve.

CHOPPING AN ONION

Chopped onions are used in many recipes, and whether they are finely or roughly chopped, the method is the same; just vary the gap between cuts to get different sized pieces.

1 Cut off the stalk end of the onion, and cut in half through the root, leaving the root intact. Remove the skin and place the halved onion, cut-side down, on the board. Make lengthwise vertical cuts into the onion, taking care not to cut right through to the root.

2 Make two or three horizontal cuts from the stalk end through to the root but without cutting all the way through.

3 Turn the onion on its side. Cut the onion across from the stalk end to the root. The onion will fall away in small squares. Cut further apart for larger squares.

PREPARING GARLIC

Don't worry if you don't have a garlic press: Try this method, which gives wonderful, juicy results.

1 Break off the clove of garlic, place the flat side of a large knife on top and strike with your fist. Remove all the papery outer skin. Begin by finely chopping the clove.

2 Sprinkle on a little table salt and, using the flat side of a large knife blade, work the salt into the garlic, until the clove softens and releases its juices. Use the garlic pulp as needed.

PREPARING CHILES

Chiles add a distinct flavor, but remove the fiery-hot seeds.

1 Always protect your hands, as chiles can irritate the skin; wear rubber gloves and never rub your eyes after handling chiles. Halve the chile lengthwise and remove and discard the seeds.

2 Slice, finely chop and use as needed. Wash the knife and board thoroughly in hot, soapy water. Always wash your hands thoroughly after preparing chiles.

PEELING TOMATOES

If you have the time, peel tomatoes before adding them to sauces or purées. This avoids rolled-up, tough pieces of tomato skin that don't soften during cooking.

1 Make a cross in each tomato with a sharp knife and place in a bowl.

2 Pour enough boiling water over them to cover them and let stand for 30 seconds. The skins should start to come off. Slightly unripe tomatoes may take longer.

3 Drain the tomatoes and peel the skin off with a sharp knife. Don't leave the tomatoes in the boiling water for too long.

CHOPPING HERBS

Chop herbs just before you use them.

1 Remove the leaves and place on a clean, dry board. Use a large, sharp cook's knife.

2 Chop the herbs, as finely or as coarsely as desired, by holding the tip of the blade on the board and rocking the handle up and down.

CUTTING JULIENNE STRIPS

Small julienne strips of vegetables make an attractive salad ingredient or garnish. Use this technique for carrots, cucumber and celery.

1 Peel the vegetable and use a large knife to cut it into 2-inch lengths. Cut a thin sliver from one side of the first piece so that it sits flat on the board.

2 Cut each piece into thin slices lengthwise. Stack the slices of vegetable and then cut through them again to make fine strips.

PREPARING SCALLIONS

Scallions make a crisp and tasty addition to salads. They are a little time-consuming to prepare, but the flavor is worth it.

1 Cut off the root of the scallion with a sharp knife. Peel off any damaged or tough leaves.

2 For an intense flavor and an attractive green color, cut the dark green part into matchsticks.

3 For a milder flavor just use the white part of the scallion, discard the root and slice thinly on a slight diagonal.

Fruit Preparation

CITRUS FRUIT

1 To peel completely, cut a slice from the top and from the base. Set the fruit base down on a work surface. Cut off the peel lengthwise in thick strips. Take the colored zest and all the white pith (which has a bitter taste). Cut following the curve of the fruit.

2 To remove the thin, colored zest, use a vegetable peeler to shave off the zest in wide strips, taking none of the white pith. Use these strips whole or cut them into fine shreds with a sharp knife. Alternatively, rub the fruit against the fine holes of a metal grater, turning the fruit so that you take just the colored zest and not the white pith. Or use a special tool, called a citrus zester, to take fine threads of zest. Finely chop the threads into tiny pieces.

3 For slices, cut the fruit across into neat slices using a serrated knife.

4 For segments, hold the fruit over a bowl to catch the juice. Working from the side of the fruit to the center, slide the knife down first one side of a separating membrane and then the other. Continue cutting out the segments.

FRESH CURRANTS

1 Pull through the prongs of a fork to remove red, black or white currants from their stalks.

APPLES AND PEARS

1 For whole fruit, use an apple corer to remove the whole core from stalk end to base.

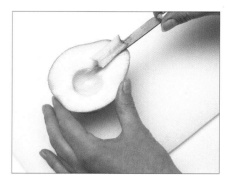

2 For halves, use a melon baller to scoop out the core. Cut out the stalk and base with a small, sharp knife. For rings, remove the core and seeds with an apple corer. Set the fruit on its side and cut across into rings.

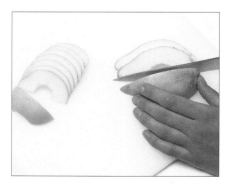

3 For slices, cut the fruit in half and remove the core and seeds with a melon baller. Set one half, cut side down, and cut it across into neat slices. Repeat with the other half.

FRESH DATES

1 Cut the fruit in half lengthwise and lift out the pit.

PAPAYAS AND MELONS

1 Cut the fruit in half. Scoop out the seeds from the central hollow, then scrape out any fibers. For slices, follow the pear technique.

KIWI, STAR FRUIT (CARAMBOLA)

1 Cut the fruit across into neat slices; discard the ends.

PINEAPPLES

1 To peel the pineapple, set the pineapple on its base, hold it at the top and cut thick slices of skin from top to bottom. Dig out any "eyes" that remain with the point of the knife.

2 For chunks, cut the peeled fruit lengthwise in half and then into quarters. Cut each quarter into spears and cut out the core.

3 Cut each spear into chunks. For rings, cut the peeled fruit across into slices and cut out the core.

KEEPING FRESH COLOR

If exposed to the air for long, the cut flesh of some fruits, such as apples, bananas and avocados, starts to turn brown. So if prepared fruit has to sit before being served, sprinkle the cut surfaces with lemon juice, or immerse hard fruits in water and lemon juice, but do not soak for long or the fruit may become soggy.

MANGOES

1 Cut lengthwise on either side of the pit. Also cut the flesh from the two thin ends of the pit.

2 Remove the skin and cut the flesh into slices or cubes.

PEACHES, NECTARINES, APRICOTS AND PLUMS

1 Cut the fruit in half, cutting around the indentation. Twist the halves apart. Lift out the pit, or lever it out with the tip of a sharp knife. Or cut the unpeeled fruit into wedges, removing the pit. Set each wedge peel side down and slide the knife down to peel.

Salad Dressings

Although the ingredients of a salad are important, the secret of a perfect salad is a good dressing. A French dressing made from the very best olive oil and vinegar can rescue even the dullest selection of lettuce leaves, while a homemade mayonnaise is always impressive. If you are a confident and experienced salad dresser you might feel able to add oil and vinegar directly to your salad just before serving, but the safest way of creating a perfect dressing is to prepare it in advance. Homemade dressings can be stored in the fridge for up to a week and will improve in flavor. Here is a selection of dressings that should be part of every cook's repertoire.

THOUSAND ISLANDS DRESSING

This creamy dressing is great with green salads and grated carrot, hot potato, pasta and rice salads.

INGREDIENTS

Makes about ½ cup

4 tablespoons sunflower oil
1 tablespoon orange juice
1 tablespoon lemon juice
2 teaspoons grated lemon rind
1 tablespoon finely chopped onion
1 teaspoon paprika
1 teaspoon Worcestershire sauce
1 tablespoon finely chopped fresh parsley
salt and ground black pepper

Put all the ingredients into a screw-top jar and season to taste. Replace the lid and shake well.

FRENCH DRESSING

French vinaigrette is the most widely used salad dressing.

INGREDIENTS

Makes about ½ cup

6 tablespoons extra-virgin olive oil
1 tablespoon white wine vinegar
1 teaspoon French mustard
pinch of caster sugar

1 Place the extra-virgin olive oil and white wine vinegar in a clean screw-top jar.

2 Add the mustard and sugar.

3 Replace the lid and shake well.

FRENCH HERB DRESSING

The delicate scents and flavours of fresh herbs combine especially well in a French dressing. Use just one herb or a selection. Toss with a simple green salad and serve with good cheese, fresh bread and wine.

INGREDIENTS

Makes about ½ cup

4 tablespoons extra-virgin olive oil
2 tablespoons groundnut or sunflower oil
1 tablespoon lemon juice
4 tablespoons finely chopped fresh herbs (parsley, chives, tarragon and marjoram)
pinch of sugar

1 Place the olive oil and groundnut or sunflower oil in a clean screw-top jar.

2 Add the lemon juice, chopped fresh herbs and sugar.

3 Replace the lid and shake well.

MAYONNAISE

Mayonnaise is a simple emulsion made with egg yolks and oil. For consistent results, ensure that both egg yolks and oil are at room temperature before combining. Homemade mayonnaise is made with raw egg yolks and may therefore be considered unsuitable for young children, pregnant mothers and the elderly.

INGREDIENTS

Makes about 1¼ cups
2 egg yolks
1 teaspoon French mustard
²⁄₃ cup extra-virgin
   olive oil
²⁄₃ cup peanut or sunflower oil
2 teaspoons white wine vinegar
salt and ground black pepper

1 Place the egg yolks and mustard in a food processor and blend smoothly.

2 Add the olive oil a little at a time while the processor is running. When the mixture is thick, add the peanut or sunflower oil in a slow, steady stream.

3 Add the vinegar and season to taste with salt and pepper.

YOGURT DRESSING

This is a less rich version of a classic mayonnaise and is much easier to make. It can be used as a low-fat substitute. Change the herbs as desired, or leave them out.

INGREDIENTS

Makes about scant 1 cup
²⁄₃ cup plain yogurt
2 tablespoons mayonnaise
2 tablespoons milk
1 tablespoon chopped fresh parsley
1 tablespoon chopped fresh chives

Put all the ingredients in a bowl. Season to taste and mix well.

BLUE CHEESE AND CHIVE DRESSING

Blue cheese dressings have a strong, robust flavor and are well suited to winter salad leaves such as escarole, chicory and radicchio.

INGREDIENTS

Makes about 1½ cups
3 ounces blue cheese (Stilton, Bleu
   d'Auvergne or Gorgonzola)
²⁄₃ cup plain yogurt
3 tablespoons olive oil
2 tablespoons lemon juice
1 tablespoon chopped fresh chives
ground black pepper

1 Remove the rind from the cheese and combine with a third of the yogurt in a bowl.

2 Add the remainder of the yogurt, the olive oil and the lemon juice.

3 Stir in the chopped chives and season to taste with ground black pepper.

BASIL AND LEMON MAYONNAISE

This luxurious dressing is flavored with lemon juice and two types of basil. Serve with all kinds of leafy salads, crudités or coleslaws. It is also good with baked potatoes or as a delicious dip for French fries. The dressing will keep in an airtight jar for up to a week in the refrigerator.

INGREDIENTS

Makes about 1¼ cups

2 large egg yolks
1 tablespoon lemon juice
⅔ cup extra-virgin olive oil
⅔ cup sunflower oil
4 garlic cloves
handful of fresh green basil
handful of fresh opal basil
salt and ground black pepper

1 Place the egg yolks and lemon juice in a blender or food processor and mix them briefly until lightly blended.

2 In a pitcher, stir together both oils. With the machine running, pour in the oil very slowly, a little at a time.

3 Once half of the oil has been added, and the dressing has successfully emulsified, the remaining oil can be incorporated more quickly. Continue processing until a thick, creamy mayonnaise has formed.

4 Peel and crush the garlic cloves and add to the mayonnaise. Alternatively, place the cloves on a cutting board and sprinkle with salt, then flatten them with the heel of a heavy-bladed knife and chop the flesh. Flatten the garlic again to make a coarse purée. Add to the mayonnaise.

5 Remove the basil stalks and tear both types of leaves into small pieces. Stir into the mayonnaise.

6 Add salt and pepper to taste, then transfer the mayonnaise to a serving dish. Cover and chill until ready to serve.

Instant Dressings and Dips

If you need an instant dressing or dip, try one of these quick and easy recipes. Most of them use pantry ingredients.

CREAM CHEESE AND CHIVE DIP

Mix 8 ounces of cream cheese with 2–3 tablespoons snipped fresh chives, and season to taste with salt and black pepper. If the dip is too thick, stir in a little milk to soften it. Use as a dressing for all kinds of salads, especially winter coleslaws.

CREAMY BLACK OLIVE DIP

Stir a little black olive paste into a carton of sour cream until smooth and well blended. Add salt, ground black pepper and a squeeze of lemon juice to taste. Serve chilled.

CRÈME FRAÎCHE DRESSING WITH SCALLIONS

Finely chop a bunch of scallions and stir into a carton of crème fraîche. Add a dash of chili sauce, a squeeze of lime juice, and salt and ground black pepper.

HERB MAYONNAISE

Liven up ready-made mayonnaise with a handful of chopped fresh herbs—try flat-leaf parsley, basil, dill or tarragon.

PASSATA AND HORSERADISH DIP

Bring a little tang to a carton or bottle of passata (sieved tomatoes) by adding some horseradish sauce or 1–2 teaspoons creamed horseradish and salt and pepper to taste. Serve with lightly-cooked vegetables.

PESTO DIP

For a simple, speedy, Italian-style dip, stir 1 tablespoon ready-made red or green pesto into a carton of sour cream. Serve with crudités or wedges of oven-roasted Mediterranean vegetables, such as bell peppers, zucchini and onions for a delicious appetizer.

SPICED YOGURT DRESSING

To make a quick, Indian-style dressing, stir a little curry paste and chutney into a carton of yogurt.

SUN-DRIED TOMATO DIP

Stir 1–2 tablespoons sun-dried tomato paste into a carton of plain

Above: Top row: creamy black olive dip, crème fraîche dressing with scallions. Second row: herb mayonnaise, yogurt and sun-dried tomato dip. Third row: yogurt and mustard dip, cream cheese and chive dip, spiced yogurt dressing. Fourth row: pesto dip, passata and horseradish dip.

yogurt. Season to taste with salt and ground black pepper.

YOGURT AND MUSTARD DIP

Mix a small carton of yogurt with 1–2 teaspoons whole-grain mustard. Serve with crudités.

LIGHT & SIDE SALADS

Crudités

A colorful selection of raw vegetables, or crudités, may be served with drinks or as small salad appetizers. The term "crudités" is used both for small pieces of vegetables served with a tasty dip and for a selection of vegetable salads presented in separate dishes. By choosing contrasting colors, it is possible to make a beautiful presentation of any combination of vegetables, raw or lightly cooked, attractively arranged on a platter or in baskets and served with a tangy dip, such as aïoli (garlic mayonnaise) or tapenade (olive paste). Allow 3–4 ounces of each vegetable per person.

AÏOLI

Put four crushed garlic cloves (or more or less, to taste) in a small bowl with a pinch of salt, and crush with the back of a spoon. Add two egg yolks and beat for 30 seconds with an electric mixer until creamy. Beat in 1 cup extra-virgin olive oil, by drops, until the mixture thickens. As it begins to thicken, the oil can be added in a thin stream until the mixture is thick. Thin the sauce with a little lemon juice and season to taste. Chill for up to 2 days; bring to room temperature and stir before serving.

TAPENADE

Put 7 ounces pitted black olives, 6 canned anchovy fillets, 2 tablespoons capers, rinsed, 1–2 garlic cloves, 1 teaspoon fresh thyme leaves, 1 tablespoon Dijon mustard, the juice of ½ lemon, ground black pepper and, if desired, 1 tablespoon brandy in a food processor fitted with the metal blade. Process for 15–30 seconds until smooth, then scrape down the sides of the bowl. With the machine running, slowly add 4–6 tablespoons extra-virgin olive oil to make a smooth, firm paste. Store in an airtight container.

RAW VEGETABLE PLATTER

INGREDIENTS

Serves 6–8

2 red and 2 yellow bell peppers, seeded and sliced lengthwise

8 ounces fresh baby corn

1 chicory head (red or white), trimmed and leaves separated

6–8 ounces thin asparagus, trimmed and blanched

1 small bunch radishes with small leaves

6 ounces cherry tomatoes

12 quails' eggs, boiled for 3 minutes, drained, refreshed and peeled

aïoli or tapenade, to serve

Arrange the prepared vegetables on a serving plate with the quails' eggs. Cover with a damp dish cloth until ready to serve. Serve with aïoli or tapenade for dipping.

TOMATO AND CUCUMBER SALAD

INGREDIENTS

Serves 4–6

1 medium cucumber, peeled and thinly sliced

5-6 ice cubes

2 tablespoons white wine vinegar

6 tablespoons crème fraîche or sour cream

2 tablespoons chopped fresh mint

4 or 5 ripe tomatoes, sliced

salt and ground black pepper

Place the cucumber in a bowl, sprinkle with a little salt and 1 tablespoon of the vinegar and toss with the ice cubes. Chill for 1 hour to crisp, then rinse, drain and pat dry. Return to the bowl, add the crème fraîche, pepper and mint and stir to mix well. Arrange the tomato slices on a serving plate, sprinkle with the remaining vinegar and spoon the cucumber slices into the center.

CARROT AND PARSLEY SALAD

INGREDIENTS

Serves 4–6

1 garlic clove, crushed

grated zest and juice of 1 orange

2–3 tablespoons peanut oil

1 pound carrots, cut into very fine julienne strips

2–3 tablespoons chopped fresh parsley

salt and ground black pepper

Rub a bowl with the garlic and leave in the bowl. Add the orange zest and juice and salt and pepper. Whisk in the oil until blended, then remove the garlic. Add the carrots and half of the parsley and toss well. Garnish with the remaining parsley.

Lettuce and Herb Salad

Stores now sell many different types of lettuce leaves year round, so try to use a mixture. Look for pre-packed bags of mixed baby lettuce leaves.

INGREDIENTS

Serves 4

½ cucumber

mixed lettuce leaves

1 bunch watercress, about 4 ounces

1 chicory head, sliced

3 tablespoons chopped fresh herbs such as parsley, thyme, tarragon, chives, chervil

For the dressing

1 tablespoon white wine vinegar

1 teaspoon prepared mustard

5 tablespoons olive oil

salt and ground black pepper

1 To make the dressing, combine the vinegar and mustard, then whisk in the oil and seasoning.

2 Peel the cucumber, if desired, then halve it lengthwise and scoop out the seeds. Thinly slice the flesh. Tear the lettuce leaves into bite-sized pieces.

3 Either toss the cucumber, lettuce, watercress, chicory and herbs in a bowl, or arrange them in the bowl in layers.

4 Stir the dressing, then pour it over the salad and toss lightly to coat the salad vegetables and leaves. Serve immediately.

Minted Melon and Grapefruit Cocktail

Melon is always a popular appetizer. Here the flavor is complemented by the refreshing taste of citrus fruit and a simple dressing.

INGREDIENTS

Serves 4

1 small Galia melon, about 2¼ pounds

2 pink grapefruit

1 yellow grapefruit

1 teaspoon Dijon mustard

1 teaspoon raspberry or sherry vinegar

1 teaspoon honey

1 tablespoon chopped fresh mint

fresh mint sprigs, to garnish

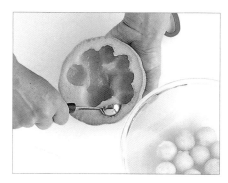

1 Halve the melon and remove the seeds with a teaspoon. With a melon baller, carefully scoop the flesh into balls.

2 With a sharp knife, peel all three grapefruit and cut off all the white pith. Remove the segments by cutting between the membranes, holding the fruit over a bowl to catch any juice.

3 Whisk the mustard, vinegar, honey, chopped mint and grapefruit juice in a mixing bowl. Add the melon balls and grapefruit segments and mix well. Chill for 30 minutes.

4 Ladle into four serving dishes, garnish each one with a sprig of fresh mint and serve.

Black and Orange Salad

This dramatically colorful salad, with its spicy dressing, is very unusual. It is a feast for the eyes as well as for the taste buds.

INGREDIENTS

Serves 4

3 oranges

1 cup pitted black olives

1 tablespoon chopped fresh cilantro

1 tablespoon chopped fresh parsley

For the dressing

2 tablespoons olive oil

1 tablespoon lemon juice

½ teaspoon paprika

½ teaspoon ground cumin

1 With a sharp knife, cut off the peel and pith from the oranges and divide the fruit into segments.

2 Place the oranges in a salad bowl and add the black olives, cilantro and parsley.

3 Blend the olive oil, lemon juice, paprika and cumin. Pour the dressing onto the salad and toss gently. Chill for about 30 minutes and serve.

Arugula and Cilantro Salad

Arugula has a wonderful, peppery flavor. However, unless you grow your own arugula, or have a plentiful supply, you may well have to use extra spinach or another green leaf in order to make this salad.

INGREDIENTS

Serves 4

4 ounces or more arugula leaves

4 ounces young spinach leaves

1 large bunch fresh cilantro, about
   1 ounce

2–3 fresh parsley sprigs

For the dressing

1 garlic clove, crushed

3 tablespoons olive oil

2 teaspoons white wine vinegar

pinch of paprika

cayenne pepper

salt

1 Place the arugula and spinach leaves in a salad bowl. Chop the cilantro and parsley and sprinkle them on the top.

2 In a small pitcher, combine the garlic, olive oil, vinegar, paprika, cayenne pepper and salt.

3 Pour the dressing onto the salad and serve immediately.

Caesar Salad

There are many stories about the origins of Caesar Salad. The most likely is that it was invented by an Italian, Caesar Cardini, who owned a restaurant in Mexico in the 1920s. Simplicity is the key to the success of this salad.

INGREDIENTS

Serves 4

3 slices day-old bread, ½-inch thick

4 tablespoons garlic oil

2-ounce piece Parmesan cheese

1 Romaine lettuce

salt and ground black pepper

For the dressing

2 egg yolks, as fresh as possible

1 ounce canned anchovy fillets, drained and roughly chopped

½ teaspoon French mustard

½ cup olive oil

1 tablespoon white wine vinegar

1 To make the dressing, combine the egg yolks, anchovies, mustard, oil and vinegar in a screw-top jar and shake well.

2 Remove the crusts from the bread with a serrated knife and cut into 1-inch fingers.

3 Heat the garlic oil in a large frying-pan, add the pieces of bread and fry until golden. Sprinkle with salt and let drain on paper towels.

4 Cut thin shavings from the Parmesan cheese with a vegetable peeler.

5 Wash the lettuce leaves and spin dry. Smother with the dressing, and scatter on the garlic croûtons and Parmesan cheese shavings. Season and serve.

COOK'S TIP

The classic dressing for Caesar Salad is made with raw egg yolks. Ensure that you use only the freshest eggs, bought from a reputable supplier. Expectant mothers, young children and the elderly are not advised to eat raw egg yolks. For them, you could omit them from the dressing and grate hard-boiled yolks on top of the salad instead.

Turkish Salad

This classic salad is a wonderful combination of textures and flavors. The saltiness of the cheese is perfectly balanced by the refreshing salad vegetables.

INGREDIENTS

Serves 4

1 Romaine lettuce heart
1 green bell pepper
1 red bell pepper
1/2 cucumber
4 tomatoes
1 red onion
2 cups feta cheese, crumbled
black olives, to garnish

For the dressing

3 tablespoons olive oil
3 tablespoons lemon juice
1 garlic clove, crushed
1 tablespoon chopped fresh parsley
1 tablespoon chopped fresh mint
salt and ground black pepper

1 Chop the lettuce into bite-sized pieces. Seed the peppers, remove the cores and cut the flesh into thin strips. Chop the cucumber and slice or chop the tomatoes. Cut the onion in half, then slice finely.

2 Place the chopped lettuce, peppers, cucumber, tomatoes and onion in a large bowl. Scatter the feta on top and toss lightly.

3 To make the dressing, blend together the olive oil, lemon juice and garlic in a small bowl. Stir in the chopped parsley and mint and season with salt and pepper to taste.

4 Pour the dressing onto the salad and toss lightly. Garnish with a handful of black olives and serve immediately.

Persian Salad

This very simple salad can be served with almost any dish. Don't add the dressing until just before you are ready to serve.

INGREDIENTS

Serves 4

4 tomatoes
1/2 cucumber
1 onion
1 Romaine lettuce heart

For the dressing

2 tablespoons olive oil
juice of 1 lemon
1 garlic clove, crushed
salt and ground black pepper

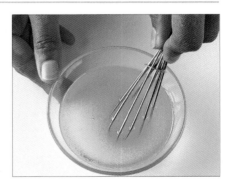

1 Cut the tomatoes and cucumber into small cubes. Finely chop the onion and tear the lettuce into pieces.

2 Place the prepared tomatoes, cucumber, onion and lettuce in a large salad bowl and combine.

3 To make the dressing, pour the olive oil into a small bowl. Add the lemon juice, garlic and seasoning and blend together well.

4 Pour onto the salad and toss lightly to mix. Sprinkle with extra black pepper and serve.

Spinach and Mushroom Salad

This nutritious salad goes well with strongly flavored dishes. If served alone as a light lunch, it could be dressed with a French vinaigrette and served with warm, crusty French bread.

INGREDIENTS

Serves 4

10 ears baby corn cobs

2 medium tomatoes

1½ cups mushrooms

1 medium onion cut into rings

20 small spinach leaves

1 ounce watercress (optional)

salt and ground black pepper

1 Halve the ears of baby corn lengthwise and slice the tomatoes.

2 Trim the mushrooms and cut them into thin slices.

3 Arrange all the salad ingredients attractively in a large bowl. Season with salt and pepper and serve.

Nutty Salad

A delicious salad with a tangy bite that can be served as an accompaniment to a main meal or as an appetizer. For wholesome finger food at a party, serve mini pita breads stuffed with the salad.

INGREDIENTS

Serves 4

1 medium onion, cut into 12 rings

¾ cup canned red kidney
   beans, drained

1 medium zucchini, sliced

1 medium summer squash, sliced

2 ounces pasta shells, cooked

½ cup cashews

¼ cup peanuts

lime wedges and fresh cilantro sprigs,
   to garnish

For the dressing

½ cup fromage frais

2 tablespoons plain yogurt

1 green chile, chopped

1 tablespoon chopped fresh cilantro

½ teaspoon crushed black peppercorns

½ teaspoon crushed dried red chiles

1 tablespoon lemon juice

½ teaspoon salt

1 Arrange the onion rings, red kidney beans, green and yellow squash slices and pasta shells in a salad dish, ready for serving. Sprinkle the cashews and peanuts on top.

2 In a separate bowl, blend together the fromage frais, yogurt, green chile, cilantro and salt and beat well using a fork.

3 Sprinkle the crushed black pepper, red chiles and lemon juice over the dressing. Garnish the salad with the lime wedges and cilantro sprigs and serve with the dressing in a separate bowl or poured onto the salad.

Fresh Cepes Salad

To capture the just-picked flavor of a cepe, this delicious salad is enriched with an egg yolk and walnut oil dressing. Choose small cepes that will have a firm texture and the very best flavor.

Serves 4

12 ounces fresh cepes

6 ounces mixed salad leaves, including batavia, young spinach and frisée

½ cup broken walnut pieces, toasted

2-ounce piece Parmesan cheese

salt and ground black pepper

For the dressing

2 egg yolks

½ teaspoon French mustard

5 tablespoons peanut oil

3 tablespoons walnut oil

2 tablespoons lemon juice

2 tablespoons chopped fresh parsley

pinch of sugar

1 To make the dressing, place the egg yolks in a screw-top jar with the mustard, peanut and walnut oils, lemon juice, parsley and sugar. Shake well.

2 Trim the cepes and cut them into thin slices.

3 Place the cepes in a large salad bowl and combine with the dressing. Let sit for 10–15 minutes for the flavors to mingle.

4 Wash and dry the salad leaves, then toss them together with the cepes.

5 Turn the cepes out onto four large serving plates. Season well, scatter on the toasted walnuts and shavings of Parmesan cheese, then serve.

Classic Greek Salad

If you have ever visited Greece, you'll know that this salad accompanied by a chunk of bread makes a delicious first course.

Serves 4

1 Romaine lettuce

½ cucumber, halved lengthwise

4 tomatoes

8 scallions, sliced

black olives

4 ounces feta cheese

For the dressing

6 tablespoons white wine vinegar

⅔ cup extra-virgin
   olive oil

salt and ground black pepper

1 Tear the lettuce leaves into pieces and place in a large bowl. Slice the cucumber and add to the bowl.

2 Cut the tomatoes into wedges and put them into the bowl.

COOK'S TIP

The salad can be assembled in advance and chilled but should be dressed only just before serving. Keep the dressing at room temperature as chilling deadens the flavor.

3 Add the scallions to the bowl with the olives, and toss well.

4 Cut the feta cheese into cubes and add to the salad.

5 Put the vinegar, olive oil and seasoning into a small bowl and whisk well. Pour the dressing onto the salad and toss to combine. Serve immediately, with extra olives and chunks of bread, if desired.

Orange and Red Onion Salad with Cumin

Cumin and mint give this refreshing salad a very Middle Eastern flavor. Small, seedless oranges are most suitable, if available.

INGREDIENTS

Serves 6

6 oranges

2 red onions

1 tablespoon cumin seeds

1 teaspoon coarsely ground black pepper

1 tablespoon chopped fresh mint

6 tablespoons olive oil

salt

fresh mint sprigs and black olives, to serve

1 Slice the oranges thinly, working over a bowl to catch any juice. Then, holding each orange slice in turn over the bowl, cut around with scissors to remove the peel and pith. Reserve the juice. Slice the onions thinly and separate into rings.

2 Arrange the orange and onion slices in layers in a shallow dish, sprinkling each layer with cumin seeds, black pepper, chopped mint, olive oil and salt to taste. Pour on the reserved orange juice.

3 Let the salad marinate in a cool place for about 2 hours. Scatter on the mint sprigs and black olives, and serve.

Spanish Salad with Capers and Olives

Make this refreshing salad in the summer when tomatoes are at their sweetest and full of flavor.

INGREDIENTS

Serves 4

4 tomatoes

½ cucumber

1 bunch scallions, trimmed
    and chopped

1 bunch watercress

8 stuffed olives

2 tablespoons drained capers

For the dressing

2 tablespoons red wine vinegar

1 teaspoon paprika

½ teaspoon ground cumin

1 garlic clove, crushed

5 tablespoons olive oil

salt and ground black pepper

1 Peel the tomatoes and finely dice the flesh. Put them in a salad bowl.

2 Peel the cucumber, dice it finely and add it to the tomatoes. Add half the scallions to the salad bowl and mix lightly. Break the watercress into sprigs. Add to the tomato mixture with the olives and capers.

3 To make the dressing, mix the wine vinegar, paprika, cumin and garlic in a bowl. Whisk in the oil and add salt and pepper to taste. Pour onto the salad and toss lightly. Serve immediately with the remaining scallions .

Carrot and Orange Salad

A fruit and a vegetable that could have been made for each other form the basis of this wonderful, fresh-tasting salad.

INGREDIENTS

Serves 4

1 pound carrots

2 large oranges

1 tablespoon olive oil

2 tablespoons lemon juice

pinch of sugar (optional)

2 tablespoons chopped pistachios or
   toasted pine nuts

salt and ground black pepper

1 Peel the carrots and grate them into a large bowl.

2 Peel the oranges with a sharp knife and cut into segments, catching the juice in a small bowl.

3 Blend together the olive oil, lemon juice and orange juice. Season with a little salt and pepper to taste, and sugar if desired.

4 Toss the orange segments with the carrots and pour the dressing on top. Sprinkle the salad with the pistachios or pine nuts before serving.

Spinach and Roasted Garlic Salad

Don't worry about the amount of garlic in this salad. During roasting, the garlic becomes sweet and subtle and loses its pungency.

INGREDIENTS

Serves 4

12 garlic cloves, unpeeled

4 tablespoons extra-virgin olive oil

1 pound baby spinach leaves

½ cup pine nuts, lightly toasted

juice of ½ lemon

salt and ground black pepper

1 Preheat the oven to 375°F. Place the garlic in a small roasting pan, toss in 2 tablespoons of the olive oil and roast for about 15 minutes, until the garlic cloves are slightly charred around the edges.

2 While still warm, transfer the garlic to a salad bowl. Add the spinach, pine nuts, lemon juice, remaining olive oil and a little salt. Toss well and add black pepper to taste. Serve immediately, inviting guests to squeeze the softened garlic purée out of the skin to eat.

Mixed Green Salad

A good combination of leaves for this salad would be arugula, radicchio, mache and curly endive, with herbs such as chervil, basil, parsley and tarragon.

INGREDIENTS

Serves 4–6

1 garlic clove, peeled

2 tablespoons red wine or sherry vinegar

1 teaspoon Dijon mustard (optional)

5–8 tablespoons extra-virgin olive oil

7–8 ounces mixed salad leaves
    and herbs

salt and ground black pepper

1 Rub a large salad bowl with the garlic clove. Leave the garlic clove in the bowl.

2 Add the vinegar, salt and pepper and mustard, if using. Stir to mix the ingredients and dissolve the salt, then whisk in the olive oil slowly.

3 Remove the garlic clove and stir the vinaigrette to combine.

4 Add the salad leaves to the bowl and toss well. Serve the salad immediately, before it starts to wilt.

VARIATION

A salad like this should always contain some pungent leaves. Try young dandelion leaves when they are in season, but be sure to pick them far away from traffic routes and agricultural crop spraying.

Apple and Celeriac Salad

Celeriac, despite its coarse appearance, has a sweet and subtle flavor. Traditionally parboiled in lemony water, in this salad it is served raw, allowing its unique taste and texture to come through.

INGREDIENTS

Serves 3–4

1½ pounds celeriac, peeled

2–3 teaspoons lemon juice

1 teaspoon walnut oil (optional)

1 apple

3 tablespoons mayonnaise

2 teaspoons Dijon mustard

1 tablespoon chopped fresh parsley

salt and ground black pepper

1 Using a food processor or coarse cheese grater, shred the celeriac. Alternatively, cut it into very thin julienne strips.

2 Place the prepared celeriac in a bowl and sprinkle with the lemon juice and the walnut oil, if using. Stir well to mix.

3 Peel the apple if desired. Cut the apple into quarters and remove the core. Slice the apple quarters thinly crosswise and toss with the celeriac.

4 Combine the mayonnaise, mustard, parsley and salt and pepper to taste. Add to the celeriac mixture and stir well. Chill for several hours until ready to serve.

Chicory, Fruit and Nut Salad

The mildly bitter taste of the attractive white chicory leaves combines wonderfully well with sweet fruit and is especially delicious when complemented by a creamy curry sauce.

INGREDIENTS

Serves 4

3 tablespoons mayonnaise

1 tablespoon yogurt

1 tablespoon mild curry paste

6 tablespoons light cream

1/2 iceberg lettuce

2 chicory heads

1/2 cup cashews

1 1/4 cups dry, shredded coconut

2 red apples

1/3 cup currants

1 Mix the mayonnaise, yogurt, curry paste and light cream in a small bowl. Cover and chill until required.

2 Tear the lettuce into pieces and put into a mixing bowl.

3 Cut the root end off each head of chicory, separate the leaves and add them to the lettuce. Preheat the broiler.

4 Broil the cashews for 2 minutes, until golden. Transfer into a bowl and set aside. Spread out the coconut on a baking sheet. Broil for 1 minute, until golden.

5 Quarter the apples and cut out the cores. Slice the apples and add them to the lettuce with the toasted coconut and cashews and the currants.

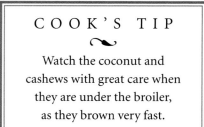

6 Spoon the dressing onto the salad, toss lightly and serve.

COOK'S TIP

Watch the coconut and cashews with great care when they are under the broiler, as they brown very fast.

Fennel, Orange and Arugula Salad

This light and refreshing salad is an ideal accompaniment to serve with spicy or rich foods.

INGREDIENTS

Serves 4

2 oranges
1 fennel bulb
4 ounces arugula leaves
⅓ cup black olives

For the dressing
2 tablespoons extra-virgin olive oil
1 tablespoon balsamic vinegar
1 small garlic clove, crushed
salt and ground black pepper

1 With a vegetable peeler, cut thin strips of zest from the oranges, leaving the pith behind. Cut the zest into thin julienne strips. Cook in boiling water for a few minutes, then drain.

2 Peel the oranges, removing all the white pith. Slice them into thin rounds and discard any seeds.

3 Cut the fennel bulb in half lengthwise. Slice across the bulb as thinly as possible, using a food processor fitted with a slicing disc. Alternatively you can use a mandoline.

4 Combine the oranges and fennel in a serving bowl and toss with the arugula leaves.

5 Combine the oil, vinegar, garlic and seasoning. Pour onto the salad, toss well and let stand for a few minutes. Sprinkle with the black olives and the julienne strips of orange and serve.

Eggplant, Lemon and Caper Salad

This cooked vegetable relish is delicious served as an accompaniment to cold meats, with pasta or simply on its own with some good, crusty bread. Make sure the eggplant is cooked until it is meltingly soft.

INGREDIENTS

Serves 4

1 large eggplant, about 1½ pounds
4 tablespoons olive oil
grated zest and juice of 1 lemon
2 tablespoons capers, rinsed
12 pitted green olives
2 tablespoons chopped fresh
    flat-leaf parsley
salt and ground black pepper

1 Cut the eggplant into 1-inch cubes. Heat the olive oil in a large frying pan and cook the eggplant cubes over medium heat for about 10 minutes, tossing regularly, until golden and softened. You may need to do this in two batches. Drain on paper towels and sprinkle with a little salt.

2 Place the eggplant cubes in a large serving bowl. Toss with the lemon zest and juice, capers, olives and chopped parsley, and season well with salt and pepper. Serve at room temperature.

> ### COOK'S TIP
> ❧
> This will taste even better when made the day before. It will keep, covered, in the refrigerator, for up to 4 days.

Apple Coleslaw

The term coleslaw stems from the Dutch koolsla, meaning "cool cabbage." There are many variations of this salad; this recipe combines the sweet flavors of apple and carrot with celery salt. Coleslaw is traditionally served with cold ham.

INGREDIENTS

Serves 4

1 pound white cabbage

1 medium onion

2 apples, peeled and cored

6 ounces carrots, peeled

⅔ cup mayonnaise

1 teaspoon celery salt

ground black pepper

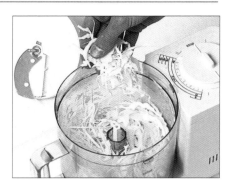

1 Discard the outside leaves of the white cabbage if they are dirty, cut the cabbage into 2-inch wedges, then remove the stem section.

2 Feed the cabbage and the onion through a food processor fitted with a slicing blade. Change to a grating blade and grate the apples and carrots. Alternatively use a hand grater and vegetable slicer.

3 Combine all the salad ingredients in a large serving bowl. Fold in the mayonnaise and season with the celery salt and black pepper.

VARIATION

For a richer coleslaw, add ½ cup grated cheddar cheese. You may find you will need smaller portions, as the cheese makes a more filling dish.

Carrot, Raisin and Apricot Coleslaw

A tasty variation on classic coleslaw, this colorful salad combines cabbage, carrots and two kinds of dried fruit in a yogurt dressing.

INGREDIENTS

Serves 6

3 cups white cabbage,
   finely shredded

1½ cups carrots, grated

1 red onion, finely sliced

3 celery stalks, sliced

generous 1 cup raisins

¾ cup dried apricots, chopped

For the dressing

½ cup mayonnaise

6 tablespoons plain yogurt

2 tablespoons chopped fresh mixed herbs

salt and ground black pepper

1 Put the cabbage and carrots in a large bowl.

2 Add the onion, celery, raisins and apricots and mix well.

3 In a small bowl, combine the mayonnaise, yogurt, herbs and seasoning.

4 Add the mayonnaise dressing to the coleslaw ingredients and toss to mix. Cover and chill for an hour before serving.

VARIATION

Use other dried fruit such as golden raisins and dried pears or peaches in place of the raisins and apricots.

Fennel Coleslaw

Another variation on traditional coleslaw in which the aniseed flavor of fennel plays a major role.

Serves 4

6 ounces fennel

2 scallions

6 ounces white cabbage

4 ounces celery

6 ounces carrots

scant ½ cup golden raisins

½ teaspoon caraway seeds (optional)

1 tablespoon chopped fresh parsley

3 tablespoons extra-virgin olive oil

1 teaspoon lemon juice

shreds of scallion, to garnish

3 Stir in the chopped parsley, olive oil and lemon juice and mix all the ingredients very thoroughly. Cover and chill for 3 hours to let the flavors mingle. Serve garnished with shreds of scallion.

VARIATION

Use sour cream instead of olive oil for a creamier dressing.

1 Using a sharp knife, cut the fennel and scallions into thin slices.

2 Slice the cabbage and celery finely and cut the carrots into fine strips. Place in a serving bowl with the fennel and scallions. Add the golden raisins and caraway seeds, if using, and toss lightly to mix.

Bean sprout and Daikon Salad

Ribbon-thin slices of fresh, crisp vegetables mixed with bean sprouts make the perfect foil for an unusual Asian dressing.

INGREDIENTS

Serves 4

1 cup bean sprouts

1 cucumber

2 carrots

1 small daikon radish

1 small red onion, thinly sliced

1-inch piece fresh ginger, peeled and cut into thin matchsticks

1 small red chile, seeded and thinly sliced

handful of fresh cilantro or mint leaves

For the dressing

1 tablespoon rice-wine vinegar

1 tablespoon soy sauce

1 tablespoon Thai fish sauce

1 garlic clove, finely chopped

1 tablespoon sesame oil

3 tablespoons peanut oil

2 tablespoons sesame seeds, toasted

1 First make the dressing. Place all the dressing ingredients in a bottle or screw-top jar and shake well. The dressing may be made in advance and will keep well for a couple of days if stored in the refrigerator or a cool place.

2 Wash the bean sprouts and drain thoroughly in a colander.

3 Peel the cucumber, cut in half lengthwise and scoop out the seeds. Peel the cucumber flesh into long ribbon strips using a potato peeler or mandoline.

4 Peel the carrots and radish into long strips in the same way as for the cucumber.

5 Place the carrots, radish and cucumber in a large, shallow serving dish, add the onion, ginger, chile and cilantro or mint and toss to mix. Pour on the dressing just before serving.

Tzatziki

Tzatziki is a Greek cucumber salad dressed with yogurt, mint and garlic. It is typically served with grilled lamb and chicken, but is also good with salmon and trout.

INGREDIENTS

Serves 4

1 cucumber

1 teaspoon salt

3 tablespoons finely chopped fresh mint, plus a few sprigs to garnish

1 garlic clove, crushed

1 teaspoon sugar

scant 1 cup plain yogurt

paprika, to garnish (optional)

1 Peel the cucumber. Reserve a little to use as a garnish if you wish and cut the rest in half, lengthwise. Remove the seeds with a teaspoon and discard. Slice the cucumber thinly and combine with the salt. Let sit for 15–20 minutes. The salt will soften the cucumber and draw out any bitter juices.

2 Place the chopped mint, garlic, sugar and yogurt in a bowl. Stir well to combine.

3 Rinse the cucumber in a sieve under cold running water to flush away the salt. Drain well and combine with the yogurt mixture in a serving bowl. Decorate with sprigs of mint. Garnish with paprika, if desired.

COOK'S TIP

If preparing tzatziki in a hurry, do not salt the cucumber. The cucumber will have a more crunchy texture and will be slightly less sweet.

Marinated Cucumber Salad

A wonderfully cooling salad for the summer, with the distinctive flavor of fresh dill.

INGREDIENTS

Serves 4–6

2 medium cucumbers

1 tablespoon salt

¹/₂ cup sugar

³/₄ cup apple cider

1 tablespoon cider vinegar

3 tablespoons chopped fresh dill

ground black pepper

1 Slice the cucumbers thinly and place them in a colander, sprinkling salt between each layer. Put the colander over a bowl and let drain for 1 hour.

2 Thoroughly rinse the cucumber under cold running water to remove excess salt, then pat dry with paper towels.

3 Gently heat the sugar, cider and vinegar in a saucepan, until the sugar has dissolved. Remove from the heat and let cool. Put the cucumber slices in a bowl, pour on the cider mixture and let marinate for 2 hours.

COOK'S TIP

This salad would be a perfect accompaniment for fresh salmon.

---

4 Drain the cucumber and sprinkle with the dill and pepper to taste. Mix well and transfer to a serving dish. Chill until ready to serve.

Flower Garden Salad

Dress a colorful mixture of salad leaves with good olive oil and freshly squeezed lemon juice, then top it with crostini.

INGREDIENTS

Serves 4–6

3 thick slices day-old bread, such as
   ciabatta

½ cup extra-virgin olive oil

1 garlic clove, halved

½ small Romaine lettuce

½ small oak-leaf lettuce

1 ounce arugula leaves or watercress

1 ounce fresh flat-leaf parsley

a small handful of young dandelion leaves

juice of 1 lemon

a few nasturtium leaves and flowers

pansy and marigold flowers

sea salt flakes and ground black pepper

1 Cut the slices of bread into ½-inch cubes.

2 Heat half the oil gently in a frying pan and fry the bread cubes in it, tossing them until they are well coated and lightly browned. Remove and cool.

3 Rub the inside of a large salad bowl with the cut sides of the garlic clove, then discard. Pour the remaining oil into the bottom of the bowl.

4 Tear all the salad leaves into bite-sized pieces and pile them into the bowl with the oil. Season with salt and pepper. Cover and keep chilled until you are ready to serve the salad.

5 To serve, toss the leaves in the oil at the bottom of the bowl, then sprinkle with the lemon juice and toss again. Scatter the crostini and the flowers on top and serve immediately.

Fresh Spinach and Avocado Salad

Young, tender spinach leaves make a change from lettuce. They are delicious served with avocado, cherry tomatoes and radishes in an unusual tofu sauce.

INGREDIENTS

Serves 2–3

1 large avocado

juice of 1 lime

8 ounces baby spinach leaves

4 ounces cherry tomatoes

4 scallions, sliced

$^1/_2$ cucumber

2 ounces radishes, sliced

For the dressing

4 ounces soft silken tofu

3 tablespoons milk

2 teaspoons mustard

$^1/_2$ teaspoon white wine vinegar

cayenne pepper

salt and ground black pepper

radish roses and fresh herb sprigs,
   to garnish

1 Cut the avocado in half, remove the pit and strip off the skin. Cut the flesh into slices. Transfer to a plate, drizzle on the lime juice and set aside.

2 Wash and dry the baby spinach leaves. Put them in a mixing bowl.

3 Cut the larger cherry tomatoes in half and add all the tomatoes to the mixing bowl with the scallions . Cut the cucumber into chunks and add to the bowl with the sliced radishes.

COOK'S TIP

Use soft silken tofu rather than the firm block variety. It can be found in most supermarkets in long-life cartons.

4 To make the dressing, put the tofu, milk, mustard, vinegar and a pinch of cayenne in a food processor or blender. Add salt and pepper to taste. Process for 30 seconds, until smooth. Scrape the dressing into a bowl and add a little extra milk if you want a thinner dressing. Sprinkle with a little extra cayenne, garnish with radish roses and herb sprigs and serve separately. Place the avocado slices with the spinach salad on a serving dish.

Radish, Mango and Apple Salad

Radish is a year-round vegetable, and this salad, with its clean, crisp tastes and mellow flavors, can be served at any time of year. Serve with smoked fish, such as rolls of smoked salmon, or with ham or salami.

INGREDIENTS

Serves 4

10–15 radishes

1 apple, peeled, cored and thinly sliced

2 celery stalks, thinly sliced

1 small ripe mango

fresh dill sprigs, to garnish

For the dressing

½ cup sour cream

2 teaspoons cream horseradish

1 tablespoon chopped fresh dill

salt and ground black pepper

1 To prepare the dressing, blend the sour cream, horseradish and dill in a small bowl and season with a little salt and pepper.

2 Trim the radishes and slice them thinly. Put in a bowl with the apple and celery.

3 Halve the mango lengthwise, cutting on either side of the pit. Make even, criss-cross cuts through the flesh of each side section and bend it back to separate the cubes. Remove the cubes with a small knife and add to the bowl. Pour the dressing onto the vegetables and fruit and stir gently so that all the ingredients are well coated. Garnish with dill sprigs and serve.

Mango, Tomato and Red Onion Salad

This salad makes a great appetizer. The under-ripe mango blends well with the tomato.

Serves 4

1 firm under-ripe mango
2 large tomatoes, sliced
½ red onion, sliced into rings
½ cucumber, peeled and thinly sliced

For the dressing
2 tablespoons sunflower or vegetable oil
1 tablespoon lemon juice
1 garlic clove, crushed
½ teaspoon hot pepper sauce
salt and ground black pepper
snipped chives, to garnish

1 Have the mango lengthwise, cutting on either side of the pit. Cut the flesh into slices and peel off the skin.

2 Arrange the mango, tomato, onion and cucumber on a large serving plate.

3 Blend the oil, lemon juice, garlic, pepper sauce and seasoning in a blender or food processor, or place in a small screw-top jar and shake vigorously.

4 Pour the dressing onto the salad and serve garnished with snipped chives.

Orange and Water Chestnut Salad

Crunchy water chestnuts combine with radicchio or red lettuce and oranges in this unusual salad.

Serves 4

1 medium red onion, thinly sliced
    into rings
2 oranges, peeled and cut into segments
1 can drained water chestnuts, peeled and
    cut into strips
2 radicchio heads, cored, or 1 red-leaf
    lettuce, leaves separated
3 tablespoons chopped fresh parsley
3 tablespoons chopped fresh basil
1 tablespoon white wine vinegar
¼ cup walnut oil
salt and ground black pepper
1 fresh basil sprig, to garnish

1 Put the onion in a colander and sprinkle with 1 teaspoon salt. Let drain for 15 minutes.

2 In a large mixing bowl, combine the oranges and water chestnuts.

3 Spread out the radicchio or red-leaf lettuce leaves in a large, shallow bowl or on a serving platter.

4 Rinse the onion to remove excess salt and dry on paper towels. Toss it with the water chestnuts and oranges.

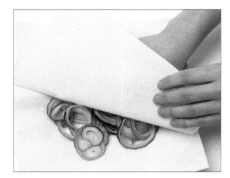

5 Arrange the water chestnut, orange and onion mixture on top of the radicchio or lettuce leaves. Sprinkle with the chopped parsley and basil.

6 Put the vinegar, oil and salt and pepper to taste in a screw-top jar and shake well to combine. Pour the dressing onto the salad and serve immediately, garnished with a sprig of basil.

Coleslaw with Pesto Mayonnaise

Both the pesto and the mayonnaise can be made for this dish. However, if time is short, you can buy them ready-prepared, and it will taste just as good. Add the dressing just before serving to keep the cabbage crisp.

INGREDIENTS

Serves 4–6

1 small or ½ medium white cabbage

3–4 carrots, grated

4 scallions, finely sliced

¼–⅓ cup pine nuts

1 tablespoon chopped fresh mixed herbs
  such as parsley, basil, chervil

For the pesto mayonnaise

1 egg yolk

about 2 teaspoons lemon juice

scant 1 cup sunflower oil

2 teaspoons pesto

4 tablespoons plain yogurt

salt and ground black pepper

1 To make the mayonnaise, place the egg yolk in a blender or food processor and process with the lemon juice. With the machine running, very slowly add the oil, pouring it more quickly as the mayonnaise emulsifies.

2 Season to taste with salt and pepper and a little more lemon juice if necessary. Alternatively, make the mayonnaise by hand using a balloon whisk.

3 Spoon 5 tablespoons of the mayonnaise into a bowl and stir in the pesto and yogurt, beating well to make a fairly thin dressing.

4 Remove the outer leaves of the cabbage and discard. Using a food processor or a sharp knife, thinly slice the cabbage and place in a large salad bowl.

5 Add the carrots and scallions, together with the pine nuts and herbs, mixing thoroughly with your hands. Stir the pesto dressing into the salad or serve separately in a small dish.

Bell Pepper and Cucumber Salad

Generous quantities of fresh herbs transform ordinary ingredients.

INGREDIENTS

Serves 4

1 yellow or red bell pepper

1 large cucumber

4–5 tomatoes

1 bunch scallions

2 tablespoons fresh parsley

2 tablespoons fresh mint

2 tablespoons fresh cilantro

2 pita breads, to serve

For the dressing

2 garlic cloves, crushed

5 tablespoons olive oil

juice of 2 lemons

salt and ground black pepper

1 Slice the pepper, discard the seeds and core. Roughly chop the cucumber and tomatoes. Place in a large salad bowl.

2 Trim and slice the scallions. Add to the cucumber, tomatoes and pepper. Finely chop the parsley, mint and cilantro and add to the bowl. If you have plenty of herbs, you can add as much as you want.

3 To make the dressing, blend the garlic with the olive oil and lemon juice in a pitcher, then season to taste with salt and pepper. Pour the dressing onto the salad and toss lightly.

4 Toast the pita bread in a toaster or under the broiler until crisp and serve it alongside the salad.

VARIATION

If you prefer, make this salad in the traditional way. After toasting the pita bread, crush it in your hand and then sprinkle onto the salad before serving.

Guacamole Salsa in Red Leaves

This lovely, light, summery appetizer looks especially attractive arranged in individual cups of radicchio leaves. Serve with chunks of warm garlic bread.

INGREDIENTS

Serves 4

2 tomatoes

1 tablespoon grated onion

1 garlic clove, crushed

1 green chile, halved, seeded and chopped

2 ripe avocados

2 tablespoons olive oil

1/2 teaspoon ground cumin

2 tablespoons chopped fresh cilantro
    or parsley

juice of 1 lime

radicchio leaves

salt and ground black pepper

fresh cilantro sprigs, to garnish

crusty garlic bread and lime wedges,
    to serve

2 Put the tomato flesh into a bowl with the onion, garlic and chile. Halve the avocados, remove the pits, then scoop the flesh into the bowl, mashing it with a fork.

3 Add the oil, cumin, cilantro or parsley and lime juice. Combine well, seasoning to taste.

4 Lay the radicchio leaves on a platter and spoon in the salsa. Serve garnished with cilantro sprigs and accompanied by garlic bread and lime wedges.

1 Using a sharp knife, slash a small cross on the top of the tomatoes, then place them in a bowl of boiling water for 30 seconds. The skins will slip off easily. Remove the core of each tomato and chop the flesh.

Thai Fruit and Vegetable Salad

A cooling, refreshing salad served with a coconut dipping sauce that has a slight kick.

INGREDIENTS

Serves 4–6

1 small pineapple

1 small mango, peeled and sliced

1 green apple, cored and sliced

6 lychees, peeled and pitted

4 ounces green beans, trimmed
  and halved

1 medium red onion, sliced

1 small cucumber, cut into short fingers

1/2 cup bean sprouts

2 scallions, sliced

1 ripe tomato, quartered

8 ounces Romaine or iceberg lettuce leaves

For the coconut dipping sauce

2 tablespoons coconut milk

2 tablespoons sugar

1/3 cup boiling water

1/4 teaspoon chili sauce

1 tablespoon Thai fish sauce

juice of 1 lime

1 To make the coconut dipping sauce, put the coconut milk, sugar and boiling water in a screw-top jar. Add the chili and fish sauces and lime juice and shake.

2 Trim both ends of the pineapple with a serrated knife, then cut off the outer skin.

Remove the central core with an apple corer. Alternatively, cut the pineapple into quarters down the middle and remove the core with a knife. Roughly chop the pineapple and set aside with the other fruits.

3 Bring a small saucepan of salted water to a boil and cook the beans for 3–4 minutes. Refresh under cold running water and set aside. To serve, arrange the fruits and vegetables in small heaps in a wide, shallow bowl. Serve the coconut sauce separately as a dip.

Sweet Cucumber Cooler

Sweet dipping sauces such as this bring instant relief to the hot chile flavors of Thai food.

INGREDIENTS

Makes about 1/2 cup

5 tablespoons water

2 tablespoons sugar

1/2 teaspoon salt

1 tablespoon rice or white wine vinegar

1/4 small cucumber

2 shallots, or 1 small red onion

1 With a small sharp knife, thinly slice the cucumber and cut into quarters. Thinly slice the shallots or red onion.

2 Measure the water, sugar, salt and vinegar into a stainless steel or enamel saucepan, bring to a boil and simmer until the sugar has dissolved, for less than 1 minute.

3 Allow to cool. Add the cucumber and shallots or onion and serve at room temperature.

Tricolor Salad

This can be a simple appetizer if served on individual salad plates, or part of a light buffet laid out on a platter. When lightly salted, tomatoes make their own flavorful dressing with their natural juices.

Serves 4–6

1 small red onion, thinly sliced

6 large full-flavored tomatoes

extra-virgin olive oil, to sprinkle

2 ounces arugula or watercress leaves, roughly chopped

6 ounces Mozzarella cheese, thinly sliced or grated

2 tablespoons pine nuts (optional)

salt and ground black pepper

1 Soak the onion slices in a bowl of cold water for 30 minutes, then drain and pat dry. Skin the tomatoes by cutting a cross in the skin and plunging into boiling water for 30 seconds. The skins can then be easily slipped off.

2 Slice the tomatoes and arrange half on a large platter or divide them among small plates.

3 Sprinkle liberally with olive oil, then layer with the chopped arugula or watercress, onion slices and cheese, sprinkling on more oil and seasoning well between the layers.

4 Season well to finish and complete with some oil and pine nuts, if desired. Cover the salad and chill for at least 2 hours before serving.

Tuscan Tuna and Bean Salad

A great dish that can be put together in very little time. Served with crusty bread, this salad is a meal in itself.

INGREDIENTS

Serves 4

1 red onion

2 tablespoons smooth Dijon mustard

1¼ cups olive oil

4 tablespoons white wine vinegar

2 tablespoons chopped fresh parsley

2 tablespoons chopped fresh chives

2 tablespoons chopped fresh tarragon
   or chervil

1 can (14 ounces) canellini beans

1 can (14 ounces) kidney beans

1 can (8 ounces) tuna in oil, drained and
   lightly flaked

fresh chives and tarragon sprigs,
   to garnish

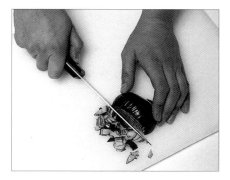

1 Chop the red onion finely, using a sharp knife.

2 To make the dressing, whisk together the mustard, oil, vinegar, parsley, chives and tarragon or chervil.

3 Drain the canellini and kidney beans in a colander, then rinse in fresh water.

4 Combine the chopped onion, beans and dressing thoroughly, then carefully fold in the tuna. Garnish with chives and tarragon sprigs and serve.

Arugula, Pear and Parmesan Salad

For a sophisticated start to an elaborate meal, try this simple salad of honey-rich pears, fresh Parmesan and aromatic arugula leaves.

INGREDIENTS

Serves 4

3 ripe pears (Williams or Packhams)

2 teaspoons lemon juice

3 tablespoons hazelnut or walnut oil

4 ounces arugula leaves

3-ounce piece Parmesan cheese

ground black pepper

2 Combine the hazelnut or walnut oil with the pears. Add the arugula leaves and toss.

3 Transfer the salad out to four small plates and top with shavings of Parmesan cheese. Season with pepper and serve.

1 Peel and core the pears and slice thickly. Moisten with lemon juice to keep the flesh white.

COOK'S TIP

Parmesan cheese is a delicious main ingredient in a salad. Buy a chunk of fresh Parmesan and shave strips off the side, using a vegetable peeler. The distinctive flavor is quite strong. Store the rest of the Parmesan uncovered in the refrigerator.

Tomato and Feta Cheese Salad

Sweet, sun-ripened tomatoes are rarely more delicious than when served with feta cheese and olive oil.

INGREDIENTS

Serves 4

2 pounds tomatoes

7 ounces feta cheese

¹/₂ cup olive oil

12 black olives

4 fresh basil sprigs

ground black pepper

2 Slice the tomatoes thickly and arrange them attractively in a shallow serving dish.

3 Crumble the feta over the tomatoes, sprinkle with oil, then sprinkle on the olives and basil sprigs. Season to taste with pepper and serve at room temperature.

1 Remove the tough cores from the tomatoes, using a small, sharp knife.

COOK'S TIP

Feta cheese has a strong flavor and can be salty. The least salty variety is imported from Greece and Turkey and is available at specialty markets.

COOKED SIDE
SALADS

~

Simple Cooked Salad

This version of a popular Mediterranean recipe is served as a side dish to accompany a main course.

Serves 4

2 well-flavored tomatoes, quartered

2 onions, chopped

½ cucumber, halved lengthwise, seeded and sliced

1 green bell pepper, halved, seeded and chopped

For the dressing

2 tablespoons lemon juice

3 tablespoons olive oil

2 garlic cloves, crushed

2 tablespoons chopped fresh cilantro

salt and ground black pepper

1 Put the prepared tomatoes, onions, cucumber and green pepper into a large saucepan, add 4 tablespoons water and simmer for 5 minutes. Let cool.

2 For the dressing, combine the lemon juice, olive oil and garlic. Strain the vegetables, then transfer to a serving bowl. Pour on the dressing, season with salt and pepper and stir in the chopped cilantro. Serve immediately, garnished with cilantro sprigs.

Sweet-and-Sour Artichoke Salad

A sweet-and-sour sauce, poured over lightly cooked summer vegetables, works perfectly in this delicious salad.

INGREDIENTS

Serves 4

6 small globe artichokes

juice of 1 lemon

2 tablespoons olive oil

2 medium onions, roughly chopped

1½ cups fresh or frozen fava beans (shelled weight)

1½ cups fresh or frozen peas (shelled weight)

salt and ground black pepper

fresh mint leaves, to garnish

For the sweet-and-sour sauce

½ cup white wine vinegar

1 tablespoon sugar

a handful of fresh mint leaves, roughly torn

1 Peel the outer leaves from the artichokes and discard. Cut the artichokes into quarters and place them in a bowl of water with the lemon juice.

2 Heat the olive oil in a large saucepan and add the onions. Cook until the onions are golden. Add the fava beans and stir, then drain the artichokes and add to the pan. Pour in 1¼ cups water and cook, covered, for another 10–15 minutes.

3 Add the peas, season with salt and pepper and cook for another 5 minutes, stirring occasionally, until the vegetables are tender. Strain through a sieve or colander and place all the vegetables in a bowl. Let cool, then cover and chill.

4 To make the sweet-and-sour sauce, mix all the ingredients in a small pan. Heat gently for 2–3 minutes, until the sugar has dissolved. Simmer gently for about 5 minutes, stirring occasionally. Let cool. To serve, drizzle the sauce onto the vegetables and garnish with mint leaves.

Tomato, Savory and French Bean Salad

Savory and beans could have been invented for each other. This salad mixes them with ripe tomatoes, making a superb accompaniment for cold meats.

Serves 4

1 pound green beans
2¼ pounds ripe tomatoes
3 scallions, roughly sliced
1 tablespoon pine nuts
4 fresh savory sprigs

For the dressing
2 tablespoons extra-virgin olive oil
juice of 1 lime
3 ounces Dolcelatte cheese
1 garlic clove, peeled and crushed
salt and ground black pepper

1 Prepare the dressing first so that it can stand for a while before use. Place all the dressing ingredients in the bowl of a food processor, season to taste and blend until the cheese is finely chopped and you have a smooth dressing. Pour it into a pitcher.

2 Trim the beans, and boil in salted water until they are just cooked.

3 Drain the beans and run cold water over them until they have completely cooled. Slice the tomatoes or, if they are fairly small, quarter them.

4 Toss the beans, tomatoes and scallions. Pour on the dressing, sprinkle the pine nuts and savory sprigs on and serve.

Squash à la Grecque

This recipe, usually made with mushrooms, also works well with patty-pan squash. Make sure that you cook the baby squash until they are quite tender, so they absorb the delicious flavors of the marinade.

INGREDIENTS

Serves 4

6 ounces patty-pan squash

1 cup white wine

juice of 2 lemons

1 fresh thyme sprig

1 bay leaf, plus extra to garnish

small bunch of fresh chervil,
    roughly chopped

1/4 teaspoon crushed coriander seeds

1/4 teaspoon crushed black peppercorns

5 tablespoons olive oil

extra bay leaves, to garnish

1 Blanch the patty-pan squash in boiling water for 3 minutes, then refresh them in cold water.

2 Place all the remaining ingredients in a pan, add 2/3 cup water and simmer for 10 minutes, covered. Add the squash and cook for 10 minutes, until they are tender. Remove with a slotted spoon.

3 Reduce the liquid by boiling hard for 10 minutes. Strain and pour it over the squash. Let sit until cool for the flavors to be absorbed. Serve cold, garnished with bay leaves.

Warm Fava Bean and Feta Salad

This medley of fresh-tasting salad ingredients is delicious warm or cold as an appetizer or accompaniment to a main course.

INGREDIENTS

Serves 4–6

2 pounds fava beans, shelled, or
    12 ounces shelled frozen beans
4 tablespoons olive oil
6 ounces fresh plum tomatoes, halved,
    or quartered if large
4 garlic cloves, crushed
4 ounces firm feta cheese, cut
    into chunks
3 tablespoons chopped fresh dill
12 black olives
salt and ground black pepper
chopped fresh dill, to garnish

1 Cook the fava beans in boiling, salted water until just tender. Drain and set aside.

2 Meanwhile, heat the olive oil in a heavy frying pan and add the tomatoes and garlic. Cook until the tomatoes are beginning to change color.

3 Add the feta to the pan and toss the ingredients for 1 minute. Mix with the drained fava beans, dill, olives and salt and pepper. Serve garnished with chopped dill.

> ### COOK'S TIP
>
> Plum tomatoes are now widely available in supermarkets fresh as well as canned. Their deep red, oval shapes are very attractive in salads, and they have a sweet, rich flavor.

Halloumi and Grape Salad

In this recipe firm, salty halloumi cheese is fried and then tossed with sweet, juicy grapes, which really complement its distinctive flavor.

INGREDIENTS

Serves 4

5 ounces mixed green salad leaves
3 ounces seedless green grapes
3 ounces seedless red grapes
9 ounces halloumi cheese
3 tablespoons olive oil
fresh young thyme leaves or fresh dill,
    to garnish

For the dressing
4 tablespoons olive oil
1 tablespoon lemon juice
½ teaspoon sugar
1 tablespoon chopped fresh thyme or dill
salt and ground black pepper

1 To make the dressing, combine the olive oil, lemon juice and sugar. Season with salt and pepper. Stir in the chopped thyme or dill and set aside.

2 Toss the salad leaves and the green and red grapes, then transfer to a large serving plate.

3 Thinly slice the cheese. Heat the oil in a large frying pan. Add the cheese and fry briefly until golden on the underside. Turn the cheese with a spatula and cook the other side.

4 Arrange the cheese on the salad. Pour on the dressing and garnish with sprigs of fresh thyme or dill.

Arugula and Grilled Goat Cheese Salad

For this recipe, look for a cylinder-shaped goat cheese or for small rolls that can be cut in half, weighing about 2 ounces each. Serve as an appetizer or a light lunch.

INGREDIENTS

Serves 4

1 tablespoon olive oil
1 tablespoon vegetable oil
4 slices green bread

For the dressing

3 tablespoons walnut oil
1 tablespoon lemon juice
8 ounces cylinder-shaped goat cheese
generous handfuls of arugula leaves
4 ounces curly endive leaves
salt and ground black pepper

For the sauce

3 tablespoons apricot jam
4 tablespoons white wine
1 teaspoon Dijon mustard

1 Heat the olive oil and vegetable oil in a frying pan and fry the slices of French bread on one side only, until lightly golden. Transfer to a plate lined with paper towels.

2 To make the sauce, heat the jam in a small saucepan until warm but not boiling. Push through a sieve into a clean pan, to remove the pieces of fruit, then stir in the white wine and mustard. Heat gently and keep warm until ready to serve.

3 Blend the walnut oil and lemon juice and season with a little salt and pepper.

4 Preheat the broiler a few minutes before serving the salad. Cut the goat's cheese in 2 ounces rounds and place each piece on a piece of French bread, untoasted side up. Place under the broiler and cook for 3–4 minutes, until the cheese melts.

5 Toss the arugula and curly endive leaves in the walnut oil dressing and arrange attractively on four individual serving plates. When the cheese croûtons are ready, arrange on each plate, pour on a little of the apricot sauce and serve.

Russian Salad

Russian salad became fashionable in the hotel dining rooms of the 1920s and 1930s. Originally it consisted of lightly-cooked vegetables, egg, shellfish and mayonnaise. Today we find it in plastic containers at supermarkets. This version recalls better days and plays on the theme of the Fabergé egg.

INGREDIENTS

Serves 4

4 ounces large button mushrooms

½ cup mayonnaise

1 tablespoon lemon juice

12 ounces shelled, cooked shrimp

1 large gherkin, chopped, or
   2 tablespoons capers

4 ounces fava beans (shelled weight)

4 ounces small new potatoes, scrubbed
   or scraped

4 ounces young carrots, trimmed
   and peeled

4 ounces baby corn

4 ounces baby turnips, trimmed

1 tablespoon olive oil

4 eggs, hard-boiled and shelled

1 ounce canned anchovy fillets, drained
   and cut into fine strips

ground paprika

salt, and ground black pepper

1 Slice the mushrooms thinly, then cut into matchsticks. Combine the mayonnaise and lemon juice. Fold the mayonnaise into the mushrooms, then add the shrimp, gherkin or capers, and seasoning to taste.

2 Bring a large saucepan of salted water to a boil, add the fava beans and cook for 3 minutes. Drain and cool under running water, then pinch the beans between thumb and forefinger to release them from their tough skins.

3 Boil the potatoes for about 15 minutes, and the remaining vegetables for 6 minutes. Drain and cool under running water. Moisten the vegetables with oil and divide among four shallow bowls.

4 Spoon on the shrimp mixture and place a hard-boiled egg in the center. Decorate the egg with strips of anchovy, sprinkle with paprika and serve.

Poached Egg Salad with Croûtons

Soft poached eggs, hot garlic croûtons and cool, crisp salad leaves make a great combination.

INGREDIENTS

Serves 2

½ small loaf white bread
⅓ cup extra-virgin olive oil
2 eggs
4 ounces mixed salad leaves
2 garlic cloves, crushed
½ tablespoon white wine vinegar
1-ounce piece Parmesan cheese
ground black pepper

1 Remove the crust from the loaf of bread. Cut the bread into 1-inch cubes.

2 Heat 2 tablespoons of the oil in a frying pan. Cook the bread for about 5 minutes, tossing the cubes occasionally, until they are golden brown.

3 Meanwhile, bring a pan of water to a boil. Carefully slide in the eggs, one at a time. Gently poach the eggs for 4 minutes, until lightly cooked.

4 Divide the salad leaves between two plates. Remove the croûtons from the frying pan and arrange them on the leaves. Wipe the frying pan clean with paper towels.

5 Heat the remaining oil in the pan, add the garlic and vinegar and cook over high heat for 1 minute. Pour the warm dressing onto each salad.

6 Place a poached egg on each plate of salad. Scatter with shavings of Parmesan and a little black pepper.

COOK'S TIP

Add a dash of vinegar to the water before poaching the eggs. This helps keep the whites together.

To ensure that a poached egg has a good shape, swirl the water with a spoon, whirlpool-fashion, before sliding in the egg.

Before serving, trim the edges of the egg for a neat finish.

Roasted Bell Pepper and Tomato Salad

A lovely, colorful recipe that perfectly combines several red ingredients. Eat this dish at room temperature with a green salad.

INGREDIENTS

Serves 4

3 red bell peppers

6 large plum tomatoes

¹/₂ teaspoon dried red chile flakes

1 red onion, finely sliced

3 garlic cloves, finely chopped

grated zest and juice of 1 lemon

3 tablespoons chopped fresh
    flat-leaf parsley

2 tablespoons extra-virgin olive oil

salt and ground black pepper

black and green olives and extra chopped
    flat-leaf parsley, to garnish

1 Preheat the oven to 425°F. Place the peppers on a baking sheet and roast, turning occasionally, for 10 minutes or until the skins are almost blackened. Add the tomatoes to the baking sheet and bake for 5 more minutes.

2 Place the peppers in a strong plastic bag, and close the top loosely, trapping in the steam. Set aside, with the tomatoes, until cool enough to handle.

3 Carefully pull the skin off the peppers. Remove the core and seeds, then chop the peppers and tomatoes roughly and place in a mixing bowl.

4 Add the chile flakes, onion, garlic, lemon zest and juice. Sprinkle on the parsley. Mix well, then transfer to a serving dish. Sprinkle with a little salt and black pepper, drizzle on the olive oil and scatter the olives and extra parsley on top. Serve at room temperature.

Marinated Zucchini

This is a simple vegetable dish that uses the best of the season's zucchini. It can be eaten either hot or cold.

INGREDIENTS

Serves 4

4 zucchini

4 tablespoons extra-virgin olive oil

2 tablespoons chopped fresh mint

2 tablespoons white wine vinegar

salt and ground black pepper

fresh mint leaves, to garnish

whole-wheat Italian bread and green
    olives, to serve

1 Cut the zucchini into thin slices. Heat 2 tablespoons of the oil in a wide, heavy-based saucepan. Fry the zucchini in batches, for 4–6 minutes, until tender and brown around the edges. Transfer the zucchini to a bowl. Season well.

2 Heat the remaining oil in the pan, then add the chopped mint and vinegar and let it bubble for a few seconds. Pour the sauce over the zucchini. Marinate for 1 hour, then serve garnished with mint leaves and accompanied by bread and olives.

Green Bean and Sweet Red Bell Pepper Salad

A galaxy of color and texture, with a jolt of heat from the chile, will make this a favorite salad.

INGREDIENTS

Serves 4

12 ounces cooked green beans, quartered

2 red bell peppers, seeded and chopped

2 scallions (both white and green parts), chopped

1 or more drained pickled serrano chiles, well rinsed, seeded and chopped

1 iceberg lettuce, coarsely shredded, or mixed salad leaves

green olives, to garnish

For the dressing

3 tablespoons red wine vinegar

9 tablespoons olive oil

salt and ground black pepper

1 Combine the green beans, peppers, scallions and chile(s) in a salad bowl.

2 To make the dressing, pour the vinegar into a bowl or pitcher. Add salt and pepper to taste, then gradually whisk in the olive oil until well combined.

3 Pour the dressing onto the prepared vegetables and toss lightly to mix and coat thoroughly.

4 Line a large serving platter with the shredded lettuce or mixed salad leaves and arrange the vegetable mixture attractively on top. Garnish with the olives and serve.

Green Green Salad

You could make this lovely dish any time of the year with frozen vegetables and still get a pretty salad.

INGREDIENTS

Serves 4

6 ounces shelled fava beans

4 ounces green beans, quartered

4 ounces snow peas

8–10 small fresh mint leaves

3 scallions, chopped

For the dressing

4 tablespoons green olive oil

1 tablespoon cider vinegar

1 tablespoon chopped fresh mint

1 garlic clove, crushed

salt and ground black pepper

1 Plunge the fava beans into a saucepan of boiling water and bring back to a boil. Remove from the heat immediately and plunge into cold water. Drain. Repeat with the green beans.

COOK'S TIP

Generally frozen fava beans are fine, but for this salad it is worth shelling fresh beans for the extra flavor.

2 In a large bowl, mix the blanched fava beans and green beans with the raw snow peas, mint leaves and scallions.

3 In another bowl, combine the olive oil, vinegar, chopped or dried mint, garlic and seasoning. Pour onto the salad and toss well. Chill until ready to serve.

Leek and Egg Salad

Smooth-textured leeks are especially delicious warm when partnered with an earthy, rich sauce of parsley, olive oil and walnuts. Serve as a side salad with plainly-grilled or poached fish and new potatoes.

INGREDIENTS

Serves 4

1½ pounds young leeks

1 egg

fresh parsley sprigs, to garnish

For the dressing

1 ounce fresh parsley

2 tablespoons olive oil

juice of ½ lemon

½ cup walnut pieces, toasted

1 teaspoon sugar

salt and ground black pepper

1 Bring a saucepan of salted water to a boil. Cut the leeks into 4-inch lengths and rinse well to flush out any grit or soil. Cook the leeks for 8 minutes. Drain and cool under running water.

2 Lower the egg into boiling water and cook for 12 minutes. Cool under running water, shell and set aside.

3 To make the dressing, finely chop the parsley in a food processor.

4 Add the olive oil, lemon juice and toasted walnuts. Blend for 1–2 minutes, until smooth.

5 Adjust the consistency with about 6 tablespoons water. Add the sugar and season to taste with salt and pepper.

6 Place the leeks on an attractive plate, then spoon on the sauce. Finely grate the hard-boiled egg and sprinkle on the sauce. Garnish with the reserved parsley sprigs and serve while the leeks are still warm.

Winter Vegetable Salad

This simple side salad is made with leeks, cauliflower and celery, flavored with white wine, herbs and juniper berries.

Serves 4

¾ cup white wine

1 teaspoon olive oil

2 tablespoons lemon juice

2 bay leaves

1 fresh thyme sprig

4 juniper berries

1 pound leeks, trimmed and cut lengthwise into 1-inch pieces

1 small cauliflower, broken into florets

4 celery stalks, sliced on the diagonal

2 tablespoons chopped fresh parsley

salt and ground black pepper

1 Put the wine, olive oil, lemon juice, bay leaves, thyme and juniper berries into a large, heavy saucepan and bring to a boil. Cover, and let simmer for 20 minutes.

2 Add the leeks, cauliflower and celery. Simmer very gently for 5–6 minutes or until just tender.

3 Remove the vegetables with a slotted spoon and transfer them to a serving dish. Briskly boil the cooking liquid for 15–20 minutes or until reduced by half. Strain through a sieve.

4 Stir the parsley into the liquid and season to taste. Pour the sauce over the vegetables and let cool. Chill for at least 1 hour before serving.

COOK'S TIP

Vary the vegetables for this salad according to the season.

Avocado and Smoked Fish Salad

Avocado and smoked fish make a good combination and, flavored with herbs and spices, create a delectable salad.

INGREDIENTS

Serves 4

2 avocados

½ cucumber

1 tablespoon lemon juice

2 firm tomatoes

1 green chile

salt and ground black pepper

For the fish

1 tablespoon butter or margarine

½ onion, finely sliced

1 teaspoon mustard seeds

8 ounces smoked mackerel, flaked

2 tablespoons fresh chopped cilantro leaves

2 firm tomatoes, peeled and chopped

1 tablespoon lemon juice

1 For the fish, melt the butter or margarine in a frying pan, add the onion and mustard seeds and fry for about 5 minutes, until the onion is soft.

2 Add the mackerel, cilantro, tomatoes and lemon juice and cook over low heat for 2–3 minutes. Remove from the heat and let cool.

3 To make the salad, slice the avocados and cucumber thinly. Place together in a bowl and sprinkle with the lemon juice. Slice the tomatoes and seed them. Finely chop the chile.

4 Place the fish mixture in the center of a serving plate.

5 Arrange the avocados, cucumber and tomatoes decoratively around the outside. Alternatively, spoon a quarter of the fish mixture onto each of four serving plates and divide the avocados, cucumber and tomatoes equally among them. Sprinkle with the chopped chile and a little salt and pepper and serve.

VARIATION

Smoked haddock or cod can also be used in this salad, or use a mixture of mackerel and haddock.

Tomato and Bread Salad

This salad, which conveniently uses up stale bread, is best made with flavorful, sun-ripened tomatoes.

INGREDIENTS

Serves 4

14 ounces stale white or brown bread
   or rolls
4 large tomatoes
1 large red onion or 6 scallions
a few fresh basil leaves, to garnish

For the dressing
4 tablespoons extra-virgin olive oil
2 tablespoons white wine vinegar
salt and ground black pepper

1 Cut the bread or rolls into thick slices. Place in a shallow bowl and soak with cold water. Let sit for at least 30 minutes.

2 Cut the tomatoes into chunks and place in a serving bowl. Finely slice the onion or scallions, and add them to the tomatoes. Squeeze as much water out of the bread as possible and add it to the vegetables.

3 To make the dressing, mix the oil and vinegar. Season with salt and pepper, pour onto the salad and mix well. Garnish with the basil leaves. Let stand in a cool place for at least 2 hours before serving.

Grilled Bell Pepper Salad

Ideally this salad should be made with a combination of red and yellow peppers for the most jewel-like, colorful effect and the sweetest flavor.

INGREDIENTS

Serves 6

4 large bell peppers, red or yellow or a
   combination of both
2 tablespoons capers, rinsed
18–20 black or green olives

For the dressing
6 tablespoons extra-virgin olive oil
2 garlic cloves, finely chopped
2 tablespoons balsamic or wine vinegar
salt and ground black pepper

1 Place the peppers under a hot broiler and turn occasionally until they are black and blistered on all sides. Remove from the heat, place in a strong plastic bag and close the top loosely. Set aside until they are cool enough to handle. Carefully peel the peppers, then cut them into quarters. Remove the stems and seeds.

2 Cut the peppers into strips, and arrange them on a serving dish. Distribute the capers and olives evenly over the peppers.

3 For the dressing, mix the oil and garlic in a small bowl, crushing the garlic with a spoon to release the flavor. Mix in the vinegar and season with salt and pepper. Pour onto the salad, mix well, and let stand for at least 30 minutes before serving.

Curly Endive Salad with Bacon

This delicious salad may also be sprinkled with chopped hard-boiled egg.

Serves 4

2 ounces white bread

8 ounces curly endive or escarole leaves

5–6 tablespoons extra-virgin olive oil

6-ounce piece bacon, diced, or
   6 thick-cut strips of bacon, cut
   crosswise into thin strips

1 small garlic clove, finely chopped

1 tablespoon red wine vinegar

2 teaspoons Dijon mustard

salt and ground black pepper

1 Cut the bread into small cubes. Tear the endive or escarole into bite-sized pieces and put into a salad bowl.

2 Heat 1 tablespoon of the oil in a medium, non-stick frying pan over medium-low heat and add the bacon. Fry gently until well browned, stirring occasionally. Remove the bacon with a slotted spoon and drain on paper towels.

3 Add another 2 tablespoons of the oil to the pan and fry the bread cubes over medium-high heat, turning frequently, until evenly browned. Remove the bread cubes with a slotted spoon and drain on paper towels. Discard any remaining fat.

4 Stir the garlic, vinegar and mustard into the pan with the remaining oil and heat until just warm, whisking to combine. Season to taste, then pour the dressing onto the salad and sprinkle with the bacon and croûtons. Serve immediately while still warm.

Asparagus and Orange Salad

*A slightly unusual combination of
ingredients with a simple dressing
based on good-quality olive oil.*

INGREDIENTS

Serves 4

8 ounces asparagus, trimmed and cut into
   2-inch lengths
2 large oranges
2 well-flavored tomatoes, cut
   into eighths
2 ounces Romaine lettuce leaves
2 tablespoons extra-virgin olive oil
$\frac{1}{2}$ teaspoon sherry vinegar
salt and ground black pepper

1 Cook the asparagus in boiling,
salted water for 3–4 minutes,
until just tender. The cooking time
may vary according to the size of
the asparagus stems. Drain and
refresh under cold water, then set
aside to cool.

2 Grate the zest from half an
orange and reserve. Peel both
the oranges and cut into segments.
Squeeze the juice from the
membrane and reserve.

3 Put the asparagus, orange
segments, tomatoes and
lettuce into a salad bowl.

1 teaspoon of the grated zest.
Season with salt and pepper. Just
before serving, pour the dressing
onto the salad and mix gently
to coat all the ingredients.

4 Combine the oil and vinegar,
and add 1 tablespoon of the
reserved orange juice and

Hard-boiled Eggs with Tuna Sauce

A tasty tuna sauce poured over hard-boiled eggs makes a nourishing first course that is quick and easy to prepare.

INGREDIENTS

Serves 6

6 extra-large eggs

1 can (7 ounces) tuna in olive oil

3 canned anchovy fillets

1 tablespoon capers, drained

2 tablespoons lemon juice

4 tablespoons olive oil

salt and ground black pepper

capers and anchovy fillets, to garnish

For the mayonnaise

1 egg yolk

1 teaspoon Dijon mustard

1 teaspoon white wine vinegar or
   lemon juice

2/3 cup olive oil

1 Boil the eggs for 12–14 minutes. Drain them under cold water. Shell the eggs carefully and set aside.

2 Make the mayonnaise by whisking the egg yolk, mustard and vinegar or lemon juice together in a small bowl.

3 Whisk in the oil a few drops at a time until 3–4 tablespoons have been incorporated. Pour in the remaining oil in a slow stream, whisking constantly.

4 Place the tuna with its oil, the anchovies, capers, lemon juice and olive oil in a blender or food processor. Process until the mixture is smooth.

5 Fold the tuna mixture carefully into the mayonnaise. Season with black pepper, and salt if necessary. Chill for at least 1 hour.

6 Cut the eggs in half lengthwise. Arrange on a serving platter. Spoon on the mayonnaise and garnish with capers and anchovy fillets. Serve chilled.

Artichoke and Egg Salad

Artichoke hearts are best when cut from fresh artichokes, but can also be bought frozen. This salad is easily assembled for a light lunch.

INGREDIENTS

Serves 4

4 large artichokes or 4 frozen artichoke
   hearts, thawed

$^1\!/_2$ lemon

4 eggs, hard-boiled and shelled

fresh parsley sprigs, to garnish

For the mayonnaise

1 egg yolk

2 teaspoons Dijon mustard

1 tablespoon white wine vinegar

1 cup olive or vegetable oil

2 tablespoons chopped fresh parsley

salt and ground black pepper

1 If using fresh artichokes, wash them. Squeeze the lemon and put the juice and the squeezed half in a bowl of cold water.

2 Prepare the artichokes one at a time. Cut off only the tip from the stem. Peel the stem with a small knife, pulling upward toward the leaves. Pull off the small leaves around the stem and continue snapping off the upper part of the dark outer leaves until you reach the taller inner leaves. Cut the tops off the leaves with a sharp knife. Place the artichoke in the acidulated water. Repeat with the other artichokes.

3 Boil or steam fresh artichokes until just tender (when a leaf comes away quite easily when pulled). Cook frozen artichoke hearts according to the package instructions. Let cool.

4 To make the mayonnaise, combine the egg yolk, mustard and vinegar in a mixing bowl. Add salt and pepper to taste. Add the oil in a thin stream while beating vigorously with a wire whisk. When the mixture is thick and smooth, stir in the chopped parsley. Blend well. Cover and refrigerate until needed.

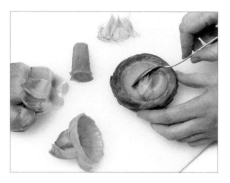

5 If using fresh artichokes, pull off the leaves. Cut the stems off level with the base. Scrape off the hairy "choke" with a knife or spoon.

6 Cut the eggs and artichokes into wedges. Arrange on a serving plate, spoon the mayonnaise on top, garnish with parsley sprigs and serve.

Panzanella

In this lively salad, a sweet, tangy blend of tomato juice, rich olive oil and red wine vinegar is soaked up by a colorful mixture of roasted bell peppers, anchovies and toasted ciabatta bread.

INGREDIENTS

Serves 4–6

8 ounces ciabatta (about ²⁄₃ loaf)

²⁄₃ cup olive oil

3 red bell peppers

3 yellow bell peppers

1 can (2 ounces) anchovy fillets, drained

1¹⁄₂ pounds ripe plum tomatoes

4 garlic cloves, crushed

4 tablespoons red wine vinegar

2 ounces capers

1 cup pitted black olives

salt and ground black pepper

fresh basil leaves, to garnish

1 Preheat the oven to 400°F. Cut the ciabatta into ³⁄₄-inch chunks and drizzle with ¹⁄₄ cup of the oil. Toast lightly until just golden.

2 Put the peppers on a foil-lined baking sheet and bake for about 45 minutes, until the skins begin to char. Remove the peppers from the oven, place in a strong plastic bag, close the end and let cool slightly.

3 Pull the skins off the peppers and cut them into quarters, discarding the stalk ends and seeds. Roughly chop the anchovies and set aside.

4 To make the tomato dressing, peel and halve the tomatoes. Scoop the seeds and pulp into a sieve set over a bowl. Using the back of a spoon, press the tomato pulp in the sieve to extract as much juice as possible. Discard the pulp and add the remaining oil, the garlic and vinegar to the juices.

5 Layer the toasted ciabatta, peppers, tomatoes, anchovies, capers and olives in a large salad bowl. Season the tomato dressing with salt and pepper and pour it onto the salad. Let stand for about 30 minutes. Serve garnished with plenty of basil leaves.

Radicchio, Artichoke and Walnut Salad

The distinctive, earthy taste of Jerusalem artichokes makes a lovely contrast to the sharp freshness of radicchio and lemon. Serve warm or cold as an accompaniment to grilled steak or barbecued meats.

INGREDIENTS

Serves 4

1 large radicchio or 5 ounces
   radicchio leaves

¹⁄₃ cup walnut pieces

3 tablespoons walnut oil

1¹⁄₄ pounds Jerusalem artichokes

thinly pared zest and juice of 1 lemon

coarse sea salt and ground black pepper

fresh flat-leaf parsley, to garnish

1 If using a whole radicchio, cut it into 8–10 wedges. Put the wedges or leaves in a flameproof dish. Sprinkle on the walnuts, then spoon on the oil and season. Toast for 2–3 minutes.

2 Peel the artichokes and cut up any large ones so that the pieces are all roughly the same size. Add the artichokes to a pan of boiling salted water with half the lemon juice and cook for 5–7 minutes, until tender. Drain. Preheat the broiler to high.

3 Toss the artichokes into the salad with the remaining lemon juice and the pared zest. Season with coarse salt and pepper. Grill until beginning to brown. Serve immediately garnished with torn pieces of parsley, if desired.

Egg, Bacon and Avocado Salad

A glorious medley of colors, flavors and textures to delight the eye and the taste buds.

INGREDIENTS

Serves 4

1 large Romaine lettuce

8 strips bacon, fried until crisp

2 large avocados, peeled and diced

6 hard-boiled eggs, chopped

2 tomatoes, peeled, seeded
   and chopped

6 ounces blue cheese, crumbled

For the dressing

1 garlic clove, crushed

1 teaspoon sugar

1/2 tablespoon lemon juice

1 1/2 tablespoons red wine vinegar

1/2 cup peanut oil

salt and ground black pepper

1 Slice the lettuce into strips across the leaves. Crumble the bacon.

2 To make the dressing, combine all the ingredients in a screw-top jar and shake well. On a large, rectangular or oval platter, spread out the strips of lettuce to make a bed.

3 Arrange the avocados, eggs, tomatoes and cheese neatly in rows on top of the lettuce. Sprinkle the bacon on top.

4 Pour the dressing carefully, and evenly onto the salad just before serving.

Spicy Corn Salad

This brilliant, sweet-flavored salad is served warm with a delicious, spicy dressing.

INGREDIENTS

Serves 4

2 tablespoons vegetable oil

1 pound drained canned corn, or frozen
   corn, thawed

1 green bell pepper, seeded and diced

1 small red chile, seeded and finely diced

4 scallions, sliced

3 tablespoons chopped fresh parsley

8 ounces cherry tomatoes, halved

salt and ground black pepper

For the dressing

1/2 teaspoon sugar

2 tablespoons white wine vinegar

1/2 teaspoon Dijon mustard

1 tablespoon chopped fresh basil

1 tablespoon mayonnaise

1/4 teaspoon chili sauce

1 Heat the oil in a frying pan. Add the corn, green pepper, chile and scallions. Cook over medium heat for about 5 minutes, until softened, stirring frequently.

2 Transfer the vegetables to a salad bowl. Stir in the parsley and the cherry tomatoes.

3 To make the dressing, combine all the ingredients in a small bowl and whisk together.

4 Pour the dressing onto the corn mixture. Season with salt and pepper. Toss well to combine, then serve immediately, while the salad is still warm.

Tofu and Cucumber Salad

A nutritious and refreshing salad with a hot, sweet-and-sour dressing, this is ideal for buffets.

INGREDIENTS

Serves 4–6

1 small cucumber

4 ounces square tofu

oil, for frying

½ cup beansprouts

salt

celery leaves, to garnish

For the dressing

1 small onion, grated

2 garlic cloves, crushed

1–1½ teaspoons chili sauce

2–3 tablespoons soy sauce

1–2 tablespoons rice wine vinegar

2 teaspoons dark brown sugar

1 Cut the cucumber into neat cubes. Sprinkle with salt to extract excess liquid. Set aside, while preparing the remaining ingredients.

2 Cut the tofu into cubes. Heat a little oil in a pan and fry on both sides until golden brown. Drain on paper towels.

3 To make the dressing, blend together the onion, garlic and chili sauce in a screw-top jar. Stir in the soy sauce, vinegar, sugar and salt to taste.

4 Just before serving, rinse the cucumber under cold running water. Drain and dry thoroughly. Toss the cucumber, tofu and beansprouts in a serving bowl and pour on the dressing. Garnish with the celery leaves and serve the salad immediately.

Plantain and Green Banana Salad

Cook the plantains and bananas in their skins to retain their soft texture. They will then absorb all the flavor of the dressing.

INGREDIENTS

Serves 4

2 firm yellow plantains

3 green bananas

1 garlic clove, crushed

1 red onion

1–2 tablespoons chopped fresh cilantro

3 tablespoons sunflower oil

1½ tablespoons malt vinegar

salt and ground black pepper

1 Slit the plantains and bananas lengthwise along their natural ridges, then cut in half and place in a large saucepan.

2 Cover the plantains and bananas with water, add a little salt and bring to a boil. Boil gently for 20 minutes, until tender, then remove from the water. When they are cool enough to handle, peel and cut into medium-sized slices.

3 Put the plantain and banana slices in a bowl and add the garlic, turning them with a wooden spoon to distribute the garlic evenly.

4 Halve the onion and slice thinly. Add to the bowl with the cilantro, oil, vinegar and seasoning. Toss to mix, then transfer to a serving bowl.

Green Bean Salad

Green beans are delicious served with a simple vinaigrette, but this dish is a little more elaborate.

INGREDIENTS

Serves 4

1 pound green beans

1 tablespoon olive oil

1 ounce butter

½ garlic clove, crushed

1 cup fresh white bread crumbs

1 tablespoon chopped fresh parsley

1 hard-boiled egg, finely chopped

For the dressing

2 tablespoons olive oil

2 tablespoons sunflower oil

2 teaspoons white wine vinegar

½ garlic clove, crushed

¼ teaspoon Dijon mustard

pinch of sugar

pinch of salt

1 Cook the green beans in boiling salted water for 5–6 minutes, until tender. Drain, refresh under cold running water and place in a serving bowl.

2 To make the dressing, thoroughly combine all the ingredients. Pour onto the beans and toss.

3 Heat the oil and butter in a frying pan and fry the garlic for 1 minute. Stir in the bread crumbs and fry over medium heat for 3–4 minutes, until golden brown, stirring frequently.

4 Remove the pan from the heat and stir in the parsley and then the egg. Sprinkle the bread crumb mixture onto the beans. Serve warm or at room temperature.

Coronation Salad

The famous salad dressing used in this dish was created especially for the coronation dinner of Queen Elizabeth II. It is a wonderful accompaniment to hard boiled eggs and vegetables.

INGREDIENTS

Serves 6

1 pound new potatoes

3 tablespoons French dressing

3 scallions, chopped

6 eggs, hard-boiled and halved

frilly lettuce leaves

¼ cucumber, cut into thin strips

6 large radishes, sliced

1 carton salad watercress

salt and ground black pepper

For the coronation dressing

2 tablespoons olive oil

1 small onion, chopped

1 tablespoon mild curry powder

2 teaspoons tomato paste

2 tablespoons lemon juice

2 tablespoons sherry

1¼ cups mayonnaise

⅔ cup plain yogurt

1 Boil the potatoes in salted water until tender. Drain them, transfer to a large bowl and toss in the French dressing while they are still warm.

2 Stir in the scallions and the salt and pepper, and let cool thoroughly.

3 Meanwhile, make the coronation dressing. Heat the oil in a small saucepan and fry the onion for 3 minutes, until soft. Stir in the curry powder, and fry for another minute. Remove from the heat and mix in all the other dressing ingredients.

4 Stir the dressing into the potatoes, add the eggs, then chill. Line a serving platter with lettuce leaves and pile the salad in the center. Sprinkle on the cucumber, radishes and watercress.

Sweet Potato and Carrot Salad

This warm salad has a sweet-and-sour taste, and several unusual ingredients. It is attractively garnished with whole walnuts, golden raisins and onion rings.

INGREDIENTS

Serves 4

1 medium sweet potato
2 carrots, cut into thick diagonal slices
3 medium tomatoes
8–10 iceberg lettuce leaves
½ cup canned chickpeas, drained

For the dressing
1 tablespoon honey
6 tablespoons plain yogurt
½ teaspoon salt
1 teaspoon ground black pepper

For the garnish
1 tablespoon walnuts
1 tablespoon golden raisins
1 small onion, cut into rings

1 Peel the sweet potato and cut roughly into cubes. Boil it until it is soft but not mushy, then cover the pan and set aside.

2 Boil the carrots for just a few minutes, making sure that they remain crunchy. Add the carrots to the sweet potato.

3 Drain the water from the sweet potato and carrots and place them together in a bowl.

4 Slice the tops off the tomatoes, then scoop out the seeds with a spoon and discard. Roughly chop the flesh. Slice the lettuce into strips across the leaves.

5 Line a salad bowl with the shredded lettuce leaves. Combine the sweet potato, carrots, chick-peas and tomatoes and place the mixture in the center.

6 To make the dressing, combine all the ingredients and beat well, using a fork.

7 Garnish the salad with the walnuts, golden raisins and onion rings. Pour the dressing on top just before serving, or serve it in a separate bowl.

COOK'S TIP

This salad makes an excellent main course for lunch or a family supper. Serve it with a sweet mango chutney and warm naan.

Potato Salads

Most people adore homemade potato salad made with a creamy mayonnaise. These two versions are lighter and more summery. The first salad should be served warm; the second can be prepared a day ahead and served cold.

Serves 4

2 pounds new potatoes

1 teaspoon salt

For the dressing for the warm salad

2 tablespoons hazelnut or walnut oil

4 tablespoons sunflower oil

juice of 1 lemon

15 pistachios, shelled

salt and ground black pepper

flat-leaf parsley, to garnish

For the dressing for the cold salad

5 tablespoons olive oil

2 teaspoons white wine vinegar

1 garlic clove, crushed

6 tablespoons finely chopped fresh parsley

2 large scallions, finely chopped

salt and ground black pepper

1 Scrub the potatoes, but don't peel them. Cover with cold water and bring to a boil. Add the salt and simmer for about 15 minutes, until tender. Drain the potatoes well and set aside.

2 For the warm salad, combine the hazelnut or walnut oil with the sunflower oil and lemon juice and season well.

3 Use a knife to crush the pistachios roughly.

4 When the potatoes have cooled slightly, pour on the dressing and sprinkle with the chopped nuts. Serve garnished with a sprig of parsley.

5 For the cold salad, cook the potatoes as above, drain and let cool.

6 Whisk together the oil, vinegar, garlic, parsley, scallions and seasoning and pour onto the potatoes. Cover tightly and chill overnight. Serve at room temperature.

Potato Salad with Egg and Lemon Dressing

Potato salads are a popular addition to any salad spread and are enjoyed with an assortment of cold meats and fish. This recipe draws on the contrasting flavors of egg and lemon. Chopped parsley provides a fresh green finish.

INGREDIENTS

Serves 4

2 pounds new potatoes

1 medium onion, finely chopped

1 hard-boiled egg

1¼ cups mayonnaise

1 garlic clove, crushed

finely grated zest and juice of 1 lemon

4 tablespoons chopped fresh parsley

salt and ground black pepper

fresh parsley sprig, to garnish

1 Scrub or scrape the potatoes, cover with cold water and bring to a boil. Add salt and simmer for 15 minutes, until tender. Drain and let cool. Cut the potatoes into large dice, season well and combine with the chopped onion.

VARIATION

Fresh chives make an excellent alternative to parsley.

2 Shell the hard-boiled egg and grate into a mixing bowl, then add the mayonnaise. Combine the garlic and lemon zest and juice in a small bowl and stir them carefully into the mayonnaise.

3 Mix the mayonnaise mixture thoroughly into the potatoes, then fold in the chopped parsley. Serve warm or cold, garnished with a sprig of parsley.

Spicy Potato Salad

This tasty salad is quick to prepare, and makes a satisfying accompaniment to grilled or barbecued meat or fish.

INGREDIENTS

Serves 6

2 pounds potatoes

2 red bell peppers

2 celery stalks

1 shallot

2 or 3 scallions

1 green chile

1 garlic clove, crushed

2 teaspoons finely snipped fresh chives

2 teaspoons finely chopped fresh basil

1 tablespoon finely chopped fresh parsley

1 tablespoon light cream

2 tablespoons sour cream

1 tablespoon mayonnaise

1 teaspoon prepared mild mustard

½ tablespoon sugar

salt

snipped fresh chives, to garnish

3 Blend the cream, sour cream, mayonnaise, mustard and sugar in a small bowl, stirring until the mixture is well combined.

4 Pour the dressing over the salad and stir gently to coat evenly. Serve, garnished with the snipped chives.

1 Peel the potatoes. Boil in salted water for 10–12 minutes, until tender. Drain and cool, then cut into cubes and place in a large mixing bowl.

2 Halve the peppers, cut out and discard the core and seeds and cut the flesh into small pieces. Finely chop the celery, shallot and scallions, and slice the chile very thinly, discarding the seeds. Add the vegetables to the potatoes together with the garlic and herbs.

Potato Salad with Garlic Sausage

*In this delicious potato salad, the
potatoes are moistened with a
little white wine before adding
the vinaigrette.*

INGREDIENTS

Serves 4

1 pound small waxy potatoes

2–3 tablespoons dry white wine

2 shallots, finely chopped

1 tablespoon chopped fresh parsley

1 tablespoon chopped fresh tarragon

6 ounces cooked garlic sausage

fresh flat-leaf parsley sprig, to garnish

For the vinaigrette

2 teaspoons Dijon mustard

1 tablespoon tarragon vinegar or white
  wine vinegar

5 tablespoons extra-virgin olive oil

salt and ground black pepper

1 Scrub the potatoes. Boil in
salted water for 10–12 minutes,
until tender. Drain and refresh
under cold running water.

2 Peel the potatoes if desired, or
leave in their skins, and cut
into ¼-inch slices. Sprinkle with
the wine and shallots.

VARIATION

The potatoes are also delicious
served on their own, simply
dressed with vinaigrette, and
perhaps accompanied by
marinated herring.

3 To make the vinaigrette, mix
the mustard and vinegar in a
small bowl, then whisk in the oil,
1 tablespoon at a time. Season and
pour over the potatoes.

4 Add the herbs to the potatoes
and toss until well mixed.

5 Slice the garlic sausage thinly
and toss with the potatoes.
Season the salad with salt and
pepper to taste and serve at room
temperature, garnished with a
sprig of parsley.

Peppery Bean Salad

*This pretty salad uses canned beans
for speed and convenience.*

Serves 4–6

1 can (15 ounces) red kidney beans

1 can (15 ounces) black-eyed peas

1 can (15 ounces) chick-peas

¼ red bell pepper

¼ green bell pepper

6 radishes

1 tablespoon chopped scallion

For the dressing

1 teaspoon ground cumin

1 tablespoon ketchup

2 tablespoons olive oil

1 tablespoon white wine vinegar

1 garlic clove, crushed

½ teaspoon hot pepper sauce

1 Drain the red kidney beans, black-eyed peas and chick-peas and rinse under cold running water. Shake off the excess water and transfer them to a large bowl.

2 Core, seed and chop the red and green peppers. Trim the radishes and slice thinly. Add the peppers, radishes and scallions to the beans.

3 Combine the cumin, ketchup, oil, vinegar and garlic in a small bowl. Add a little salt and hot pepper sauce to taste and stir again thoroughly.

4 Pour the dressing over the salad and mix. Chill the salad for at least 1 hour before serving, garnished with the sliced scallion.

Ham and Bean Salad

A fairly substantial salad that should be served in small quantities if intended as an accompaniment.

INGREDIENTS

Serves 8

6 ounces black-eyed peas
1 onion
1 carrot
8 ounces cooked ham, diced
3 medium tomatoes, peeled, seeded
   and diced
salt and ground black pepper

For the dressing
2 garlic cloves, crushed
3 tablespoons olive oil
3 tablespoons red wine vinegar
2 tablespoons vegetable oil
1 tablespoon lemon juice
1 tablespoon chopped fresh or
   1 teaspoon dried basil
1 tablespoon whole grain mustard
1 teaspoon soy sauce
½ teaspoon dried oregano
½ teaspoon sugar
¼ teaspoon Worcestershire sauce
½ teaspoon chili sauce

1 Soak the beans in cold water to cover overnight. Drain.

2 Put the beans in a large saucepan and add the onion and carrot. Cover with fresh cold water and bring to a boil. Lower the heat and simmer for about 1 hour, until the beans are tender.

3 Drain the beans, reserving the onion and carrot. Transfer the beans to a salad bowl.

4 Finely chop the onion and carrot. Toss with the beans. Stir in the ham and tomatoes.

5 For the dressing, combine all the ingredients in a small bowl and whisk to mix.

6 Pour the dressing over the ham and beans. Season with salt and pepper. Toss to combine, then serve.

White Bean and Celery Salad

This simple bean salad is a delicious alternative to the potato salad that seems to appear on every salad menu. If you do not have time to soak and cook dried beans, you can use canned ones.

INGREDIENTS

Serves 4

1 pound dried white beans (canellini, navy or butter beans) or 3 cans (14 ounces) white beans
4 cups vegetable stock
3 celery stalks, cut into ½-inch strips
½ cup French Dressing
3 tablespoons chopped fresh parsley
salt and ground black pepper

1 If you are using dried beans, cover them with plenty of cold water and soak for at least 4 hours. Discard the soaking water, then place the beans in a heavy saucepan. Cover with water.

2 Bring to a boil and simmer without a lid for 1½ hours, or until the skins are broken. Cooked beans will squash readily between a thumb and forefinger. Drain the beans. If using canned beans, drain and rinse.

3 Place the cooked beans in a large saucepan. Add the vegetable stock and celery, bring to a boil, cover and simmer for 15 minutes. Drain thoroughly. Moisten the beans with the French dressing, and let cool.

4 Add the chopped parsley and mix. Season to taste with salt and pepper, transfer to a salad bowl and serve.

Lentil and Cabbage Salad

A warm salad that makes a satisfying meal if served with crusty French bread or whole-wheat rolls.

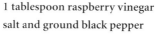
INGREDIENTS

Serves 4–6

1 cup puy lentils

3 garlic cloves

1 bay leaf

1 small onion, peeled and studded with
   2 cloves

1 tablespoon olive oil

1 red onion, finely sliced

1 tablespoon fresh thyme leaves

12 ounces cabbage, finely shredded

finely grated zest and juice of 1 lemon

1 tablespoon raspberry vinegar

salt and ground black pepper

1 Rinse the lentils in cold water and place in a large pan with 6¼ cups cold water, 1 of the garlic cloves, the bay leaf and clove-studded onion. Bring to a boil and cook for 10 minutes. Reduce the heat, cover and simmer gently for 15–20 minutes. Drain and discard the onion, garlic and bay leaf.

2 Crush the remaining garlic cloves. Heat the oil in a large pan. Add the red onion, crushed garlic and thyme and cook for 5 minutes, until softened.

3 Add the cabbage and cook for 3–5 minutes, until just cooked but still crisp.

4 Stir in the cooked lentils, lemon zest and juice and the raspberry vinegar. Season to taste and serve warm.

Brown Bean Salad

*Brown beans, sometimes called
ful medames, are available at
healthfood stores and Middle
Eastern grocery stores. Dried fava
beans or kidney beans make a
good substitute.*

INGREDIENTS

Serves 6

1½ cups dried brown beans

3 fresh thyme sprigs

2 bay leaves

1 onion, halved

4 garlic cloves, crushed

1½ teaspoons crushed cumin seeds

3 scallions, finely chopped

6 tablespoons chopped fresh parsley

4 teaspoons lemon juice

6 tablespoons olive oil

3 hard-boiled eggs, roughly chopped

1 dill pickle, roughly chopped

salt and ground black pepper

1 Put the beans in a bowl with plenty of cold water, and let soak overnight. Drain, transfer to a saucepan and cover with fresh water. Bring to a boil and boil rapidly for 10 minutes.

2 Reduce the heat and add the thyme, bay leaves and onion. Simmer very gently for about 1 hour, until tender. Drain and discard the herbs and onion.

COOK'S TIP

The cooking time for dried
beans can vary considerably.
They may need only 45 minutes
or a lot longer.

3 Place the beans in a large bowl. Combine the garlic, cumin seeds, scallions, parsley, lemon juice and oil in a small bowl, and add a little salt and pepper. Pour this over the beans and toss the ingredients lightly.

4 Gently stir in the eggs and dill pickle. Transfer the salad to a serving dish, and serve immediately.

Cracked Wheat Salad

Fresh herbs, bursting with the flavors of summer, are essential for this salad. Dried herbs will not make a suitable substitute.

INGREDIENTS

Serves 4

1⅓ cups cracked wheat

1½ cups vegetable stock

1 cinnamon stick

generous pinch of ground cumin

pinch of cayenne pepper

pinch of ground cloves

1 teaspoon salt

10 snow peas, trimmed

1 red and 1 yellow bell pepper, roasted, skinned, seeded and diced

2 plum tomatoes, peeled, seeded and diced

2 shallots, finely sliced

5 black olives, pitted and cut into quarters

2 tablespoons each shredded fresh basil, mint and parsley

2 tablespoons roughly chopped walnuts

2 tablespoons balsamic vinegar

½ cup extra-virgin olive oil

ground black pepper

onion rings, to garnish

1 Place the cracked wheat in a large bowl. Pour the stock into a saucepan and bring to a boil with the spices and salt.

2 Cook for 1 minute, then pour the stock, with the cinnamon stick, over the cracked wheat. Let stand for 30 minutes.

3 In another bowl, combine the snow peas, peppers, tomatoes, shallots, olives, herbs and walnuts. Add the vinegar, olive oil and a little black pepper and stir thoroughly to mix.

4 Strain the cracked wheat and discard the cinnamon stick. Place the cracked wheat in a serving bowl, stir in the fresh vegetable mixture and serve, garnished with onion rings.

Fruited Brown Rice Salad

An Asian-style dressing accompanies this salad. Brown rice has a nuttier flavor than white rice.

INGREDIENTS

Serves 4–6

²/₃ cup brown rice

1 small red bell pepper, seeded and diced

1 can (7 ounces) corn niblets, drained

3 tablespoons golden raisins

1 can (8 ounces) pineapple chunks in juice

1 tablespoon soy sauce

1 tablespoon sunflower oil

1 tablespoon hazelnut oil

1 garlic clove, crushed

1 teaspoon finely chopped fresh ginger

salt and ground black pepper

4 scallions, sliced, to garnish

1 Cook the brown rice in a large saucepan of lightly salted boiling water for about 30 minutes or until it is tender. Drain thoroughly and cool. Meanwhile, prepare the garnish. Slice the scallions at an angle, as shown, then set aside.

2 Transfer the rice to a large serving bowl and add the red pepper, corn and golden raisins. Drain the pineapple pieces, reserving the juice, then add them to the rice mixture and toss lightly.

3 Pour the reserved pineapple juice into a clean screw-top jar. Add the soy sauce, sunflower and hazelnut oils, garlic and ginger. Season with salt and pepper. Close the jar tightly and shake well to combine.

4 Pour the dressing onto the salad and toss well. Sprinkle the scallions on top and serve.

COOK'S TIP

Hazelnut oil gives a wonderfully distinctive flavor to any salad dressing. Like olive oil, it contains mainly mono-unsaturated fats.

Couscous Salad

There are many ways of serving couscous. This salad has a delicate flavor and is excellent with grilled chicken or kebabs.

INGREDIENTS

Serves 4

1²/₃ cups couscous

2¼ cups boiling vegetable stock

16–20 black olives

2 small zucchini

¼ cup sliced almonds, toasted

4 tablespoons olive oil

1 tablespoon lemon juice

1 tablespoon chopped fresh cilantro

1 tablespoon chopped fresh parsley

good pinch of ground cumin

good pinch of cayenne pepper

salt

3 Carefully mix the zucchini, olives and toasted almonds into the couscous.

4 Combine the olive oil, lemon juice, herbs, spices and a pinch of salt in a small pitcher or bowl. Stir into the salad.

1 Place the couscous in a bowl and pour in the boiling stock. Stir with a fork and then set aside for 10 minutes for the stock to be absorbed. Fluff up with a fork.

2 Halve the olives, discarding the pits. Trim the zucchini, and cut them into small julienne strips.

Orange and Cracked Wheat Salad

*Cracked wheat makes an excellent
alternative to rice or pasta as a
filling side salad.*

INGREDIENTS

Serves 4

1 small green bell pepper

scant 1 cup cracked wheat

¼ cucumber, diced

½ cup chopped fresh mint

⅓ cup sliced almonds, toasted

grated zest and juice of 1 lemon

2 seedless oranges, peeled

salt and ground black pepper

fresh mint sprigs, to garnish

1 Using a sharp vegetable knife,
carefully halve and seed the
green pepper. Cut into small cubes,
and set aside.

2 Place the cracked wheat in a
saucepan and add 2½ cups
water. Bring to a boil, lower the
heat, cover and simmer for
10–15 minutes, until tender.
Alternatively, place the cracked
wheat in a heatproof bowl, pour
in boiling water, and let soak for
30 minutes. Most, if not all, of the
water should be absorbed; drain
off any excess.

3 Toss the cracked wheat with
the cucumber, green pepper,
mint and toasted almonds in a
serving bowl. Add the grated
lemon zest and juice.

4 Working over the salad bowl to
catch the juice, cut the oranges
into neat segments, leaving the
membrane behind. Add the
segments to the cracked wheat
mixture, then season with salt and
pepper and toss lightly. Garnish
with mint sprigs and serve.

VARIATION:
CRACKED WHEAT SALAD
WITH FENNEL AND
POMEGRANATE

This version uses the added
crunchiness of fennel and the
sweetness of pomegranate seeds.
Perfect for a summer lunch.

INGREDIENTS

Serves 6

1⅓ cups cracked wheat

2 fennel bulbs

1 small red chile, seeded and
    finely chopped

1 celery stalk, finely sliced

2 tablespoons olive oil

finely grated zest and juice of 2 lemons

6–8 scallions, chopped

6 tablespoons chopped fresh mint

6 tablespoons chopped fresh parsley

the seeds from 1 pomegranate

salt and ground black pepper

lettuce leaves, to serve

1 Place the bulgur wheat in a
bowl and pour in boiling water
to cover. Let stand for 30 minutes.

2 Drain through a sieve,
pressing out excess water.

3 Halve the fennel bulbs and cut
into very fine slices.

4 Combine all the remaining
ingredients, then stir in the
bulgur wheat and fennel. Season
well, cover and set aside for
30 minutes before serving with
lettuce leaves.

MAIN COURSE
SALADS

~

Salade Niçoise

Served with good French bread, this regional classic makes a wonderful summer lunch or light supper dish.

INGREDIENTS

Serves 4–6

8 ounces green beans

1 pound new potatoes, peeled and
    cut into 1-inch pieces

white wine vinegar and olive oil,
    for sprinkling

1 small Romaine or round lettuce, torn
    into bite-sized pieces

4 ripe plum tomatoes, quartered

1 small cucumber, peeled, seeded
    and diced

1 green or red bell pepper, seeded and
    thinly sliced

4 hard-boiled eggs, peeled and quartered

24 black olives

1 can (8 ounces) tuna in water, drained

1 can (2 ounces) anchovy fillets in olive
    oil, drained

basil leaves, to garnish

garlic croûtons, to serve

For the anchovy vinaigrette

4 teaspoons Dijon mustard

1 can (2 ounces) anchovy fillets in olive
    oil, drained

1 garlic clove, crushed

4 tablespoons lemon juice or white
    wine vinegar

½ cup sunflower oil

½ cup extra-virgin olive oil

ground black pepper

1 First, make the anchovy vinaigrette. Place the mustard, anchovies and garlic in a bowl and combine by pressing the garlic and anchovies against the sides of the bowl. Season generously with pepper. Using a small whisk, blend in the lemon juice or vinegar. Slowly whisk in the sunflower oil in a thin stream, followed by the olive oil, whisking until the dressing is smooth and creamy.

2 Alternatively, put all the ingredients except the oils in a food processor fitted with the metal blade and process to combine. With the machine running, slowly add the oils in a thin stream until the vinaigrette is thick and creamy.

3 Drop the green beans into a large saucepan of boiling water and boil for 3 minutes until tender, yet crisp. Transfer the beans to a colander with a slotted spoon, then rinse under cold running water. Drain again and set aside.

4 Add the potatoes to the same boiling water, reduce the heat and simmer for 10–15 minutes, until just tender, then drain. Sprinkle with a little vinegar and olive oil and a spoonful of the vinaigrette.

5 Arrange the lettuce on a serving platter, top with the tomatoes, cucumber and red or green pepper, then add the green beans and potatoes.

6 Arrange the eggs around the edge. Place olives, tuna and anchovies on top and garnish with the basil leaves. Drizzle with the remaining vinaigrette and serve with garlic croûtons.

COOK'S TIP

To make garlic croûtons, thinly slice a loaf of French bread or a larger loaf, such as rustic country bread, into 1-inch cubes. Place the bread in a single layer on a baking sheet and cook in the oven, preheated to 350°F, for 7–10 minutes or until golden, turning once. Rub the toast with a garlic clove and serve hot, or allow to cool and store in an airtight container.

Moroccan Tuna Salad

This salad is similar to the classic Salade Niçoise but uses tuna or swordfish steaks and fresh fava beans along with the familiar green beans.

INGREDIENTS

Serves 6

about 2 pounds fresh tuna or swordfish, sliced into ¾-inch steaks
olive oil, for brushing

For the salad
1 pound green beans, trimmed
1 pound fava beans
1 Romaine lettuce
1 pound cherry tomatoes, halved, unless very tiny
2 tablespoons coarsely chopped fresh cilantro
3 hard-boiled eggs
3 tablespoons olive oil
2–3 teaspoons lime or lemon juice
½ garlic clove, crushed
1½–2 cups pitted black olives

For the marinade
1 onion
2 garlic cloves
½ bunch fresh parsley
½ bunch fresh cilantro
2 teaspoons paprika
3 tablespoons olive oil
2 tablespoons white wine vinegar
1 tablespoon lime or lemon juice

1 First make the marinade. Place all the ingredients in a food processor, add 3 tablespoons water and process for 30–40 seconds, until finely chopped.

2 Prick the tuna or swordfish steaks all over with a fork, place in a shallow dish and pour on the marinade, turning the fish so that each piece is well coated. Cover with plastic wrap and set aside in a cool place for 2–4 hours.

3 To prepare the salad, cook the green beans and fava beans in boiling salted water until tender. Drain and refresh under cold water. Discard the outer shells from the fava beans, and place in a large serving bowl with the green beans.

4 Discard the outer lettuce leaves and tear the inner leaves into pieces. Add to the salad with the tomatoes and cilantro. Shell the eggs and cut into eighths. Mix the olive oil, lime or lemon juice and garlic to make a dressing.

5 Preheat the broiler, and arrange the tuna or swordfish steaks in a broiler pan. Brush with the marinade and a little extra olive oil and broil for 5–6 minutes on each side, until the fish is tender and flakes easily. Brush with marinade and more olive oil when turning the fish over.

6 Let the fish cool a little then break the steaks into large pieces. Toss into the salad with the olives and the dressing. Decorate with the eggs and serve.

Warm Fish Salad with Mango Dressing

This salad is best served during the summer months, preferably outside. The dressing combines the flavor of rich mango with hot chile, ginger and lime.

INGREDIENTS

Serves 4

1 loaf French bread

4 redfish, black bream or porgy, each about 10 ounces

1 tablespoon vegetable oil

1 mango

½-inch piece fresh ginger

1 red chile, seeded and finely chopped

2 tablespoons lime juice

2 tablespoons chopped fresh cilantro

6 ounces baby spinach

5 ounces bok choy

6 ounces cherry tomatoes, halved

1 Preheat the oven to 350°F. Cut the French bread into 8-inch pieces. Slice lengthwise, then cut into thick fingers. Place the bread on a baking sheet, and let dry in the oven for 15 minutes.

2 Preheat the grill or light the barbecue and allow the embers to settle. Slash the fish deeply on both sides and moisten with oil. Grill or barbecue the fish for 6 minutes, turning once.

3 Peel the mango and cut in half, discarding the stone. Thinly slice one half and set aside. Place the other half in a food processor. Peel the ginger, grate finely, then add to the mango with the chile, lime juice and coriander. Process until smooth. Adjust to a pouring consistency with 2–3 tablespoons water.

4 Wash the spinach and bok choy leaves and spin dry, then distribute them among four serving plates. Place the fish over the leaves. Spoon on the mango dressing and finish with the reserved slices of mango and the tomato halves. Serve with the fingers of crispy French bread.

Grilled Salmon and Spring Vegetable Salad

Spring is the time to enjoy sweet, young vegetables. Cook them briefly, cool to room temperature, dress and serve with a piece of lightly grilled salmon topped with sorrel and quail's eggs.

INGREDIENTS

Serves 4

12 ounces small new potatoes, scrubbed
    or scraped
4 quail's eggs
4 ounces young carrots, peeled
4 ounces baby corn
4 ounces sugar snap peas, trimmed
4 ounces green beans, trimmed
4 ounces baby zucchini
4 ounces patty-pan squash (optional)
½ cup French Dressing
4 salmon fillets, each about 5 ounces,
    skinned
4 ounces sorrel, stems removed
salt and ground black pepper

2 Cover the quail's eggs with boiling water and cook for 8 minutes. Refresh under cold water, shell and cut in half.

4 Brush the salmon fillets with some of the French Dressing and grill for 6 minutes, turning once.

3 Bring a saucepan of salted water to a boil, add the carrots, corn, sugar snap peas, beans, zucchini and squash, if using, and cook for 2–3 minutes. Drain well. Place the hot vegetables and potatoes in a bowl, moisten with a little French Dressing and let cool.

5 Place the sorrel in a stainless-steel or enamel saucepan with 2 tablespoons French Dressing. Cover and soften over low heat for 2 minutes. Strain and cool to room temperature.

6 Divide the potatoes and vegetables among four large serving plates, then position a piece of salmon on one side of each plate. Place a spoonful of sorrel on each piece of salmon and top with two pieces of quail's egg. Season and serve at room temperature.

1 Bring the potatoes to a boil in salted water and cook for about 15 minutes, until tender. Drain, cover and keep warm.

VARIATION

If sorrel is unavailable, use baby spinach leaves instead. Cook it gently in the same way as the sorrel.

Noodles with Pineapple, Ginger and Chiles

A coconut, lime and fish sauce dressing is the perfect partner to this fruity and spicy salad.

INGREDIENTS

Serves 4

10 ounces dried udon noodles

½ pineapple, peeled, cored and sliced into 1½-inch rings

3 tablespoons light brown sugar

4 tablespoons lime juice

4 tablespoons coconut milk

2 tablespoons Thai fish sauce

2 tablespoons grated fresh ginger

2 garlic cloves, finely chopped

1 ripe mango or 2 peaches, finely diced

ground black pepper

2 scallions, finely sliced, 2 red chiles, seeded and finely shredded, and fresh mint leaves, to garnish

1 Cook the noodles in a large saucepan of boiling water until tender, following the directions on the package. Drain, refresh under cold water and drain again.

2 Place the pineapple rings in a flameproof dish, sprinkle with 2 tablespoons of the sugar and broil for about 5 minutes or until golden. Cool slightly and cut into small dice.

3 Mix the lime juice, coconut milk and fish sauce in a salad bowl. Add the remaining brown sugar with the ginger, garlic and black pepper and whisk well. Add the noodles and pineapple.

4 Add the mango or peaches and toss. Sprinkle on the scallions, chiles and mint leaves before serving.

Buckwheat Noodles with Smoked Salmon

Young pea sprouts are available for only a short time. You can substitute watercress, young leeks or your favorite green vegetable or herb in this dish.

INGREDIENTS

Serves 4

8 ounces buckwheat or soba noodles

1 tablespoon oyster sauce

juice of ½ lemon

2–3 tablespoons light olive oil

4 ounces smoked salmon, cut into fine strips

4 ounces young pea sprouts

2 ripe tomatoes, peeled, seeded and cut into strips

1 tablespoon snipped chives

ground black pepper

1 Cook the buckwheat or soba noodles in a large saucepan of boiling water until tender, following the directions on the package. Drain, then rinse under cold running water and drain well.

2 Transfer the noodles to a large bowl. Add the oyster sauce and lemon juice and season with pepper to taste. Moisten the noodles with the olive oil.

3 Add the smoked salmon, pea sprouts, tomatoes and chives. Mix well and serve immediately.

Smoked Trout and Noodle Salad

It is important to use ripe, juicy tomatoes for this fresh-tasting salad. For a special occasion you could use smoked salmon.

INGREDIENTS

Serves 4

8 ounces ramen noodles

2 smoked trout, skinned and boned

2 hard-boiled eggs, coarsely chopped

2 tablespoons snipped fresh chives

lime halves, to serve (optional)

For the dressing

6 ripe plum tomatoes

2 shallots, finely chopped

2 tablespoons tiny capers, rinsed

2 tablespoons chopped fresh tarragon

finely grated zest and juice of ½ orange

4 tablespoons extra-virgin olive oil

salt and ground black pepper

1 To make the dressing, cut the tomatoes in half, remove the cores and cut the flesh into chunks.

2 Place in a bowl with the shallots, capers, tarragon, orange zest and juice and olive oil. Season with salt and pepper and mix well. Let marinate at room temperature for 1–2 hours.

3 Cook the noodles in a large saucepan of boiling water, following the directions on the package, until just tender. Drain and rinse under cold running water. Drain well.

4 Toss the noodles with the dressing, then adjust the seasoning to taste. Arrange the noodles on a large serving platter or individual plates.

5 Flake the smoked trout onto the noodles, then sprinkle the eggs and chives on top. Serve with lime halves on the side of the plate, if desired.

Smoked Trout and Horseradish Salad

In the summer, when lettuce leaves are sweet and crisp, partner them with fillets of smoked trout, warm new potatoes and a creamy horseradish dressing.

INGREDIENTS

Serves 4

1½ pounds new potatoes

4 smoked trout fillets

4 ounces mixed lettuce leaves

4 slices dark rye bread, cut into fingers

salt and ground black pepper

For the dressing

4 tablespoons horseradish

4 tablespoons peanut oil

1 tablespoon white wine vinegar

2 teaspoons caraway seeds

1 Scrub the potatoes. Bring to a boil in a saucepan of salted water and simmer for about 15 minutes, until tender. Remove the skin from the trout fillets and lift the flesh from the bone.

COOK'S TIP

In some cases it is better to season the leaves rather than the dressing when making a salad.

2 To make the dressing, place all the ingredients in a screw-top jar and shake vigorously. Season the lettuce leaves and moisten them with the dressing. Distribute among four serving plates.

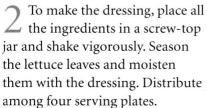

3 Flake the trout fillets and cut the potatoes in half. Sprinkle them and the rye bread fingers onto the salad leaves and toss. Season the salad to taste and serve.

Shrimp and Artichoke Salad

The mild flavors of shrimp and artichoke hearts are complemented by a tangy herb dressing.

INGREDIENTS

Serves 4

1 garlic clove

2 teaspoons Dijon mustard

4 tablespoons red wine vinegar

⅔ cup olive oil

3 tablespoons shredded fresh basil leaves
   or 2 tablespoons finely chopped
   fresh parsley

1 red onion, very finely sliced

12 ounces shelled cooked shrimp

1 can (14 ounces) artichoke hearts

½ iceberg lettuce

salt and ground black pepper

1 Chop the garlic, then crush it to a pulp with 1 teaspoon salt, using the flat edge of a heavy knife blade. Mix the garlic and mustard to a paste in a small bowl.

2 Beat in the vinegar and finally the olive oil, beating hard to make a thick, creamy dressing. Season with black pepper and, if necessary, additional salt.

3 Stir the basil or parsley into the dressing, followed by the sliced onion. Let stand for 30 minutes at room temperature, then stir in the shrimp and refrigerate for 1 hour or until ready to serve.

4 Drain the artichoke hearts and halve each one. Shred the lettuce finely.

5 Make a bed of lettuce on a serving platter or four individual salad plates and spread the artichoke hearts over it.

6 Immediately before serving, pour the shrimp and their marinade on top of the salad.

Ghanaian Shrimp Salad

The addition of plantain, which is first cooked in its skin, brings an unusual flavor to this salad.

INGREDIENTS

Serves 4

4 ounces shelled shrimp
1 garlic clove, crushed
½ teaspoon vegetable oil
2 eggs
1 yellow plantain, halved
4 lettuce leaves
2 tomatoes
1 red bell pepper, seeded
1 avocado
juice of 1 lemon
1 carrot
1 can (7 ounces) tuna or sardines, drained
1 green chile, finely chopped
2 tablespoons chopped scallion
salt and ground black pepper

1 Put the shrimp and garlic in a small bowl. Add a little seasoning.

2 Heat the oil in a small saucepan, add the shrimp and cook over low heat for a few minutes. Transfer to a plate to cool.

VARIATION

To vary this salad, use other types of canned fish and a mixture of interesting lettuce leaves.

3 Hard-boil the eggs, place in cold water to cool, then shell and cut into slices.

4 Boil the unpeeled plantain in a pan of water for 15 minutes, cool, then peel and cut into thick slices.

5 Shred the lettuce and arrange on a large serving plate. Slice the tomatoes and red pepper and peel and slice the avocado, sprinkling it with a little lemon juice.

6 Cut the carrot into matchstick-size pieces and arrange on the lettuce with the other vegetables.

7 Add the plantain, eggs, shrimp and tuna or sardines. Sprinkle with the remaining lemon juice, scatter the chile and scallion on top, season and serve.

Shrimp Salad with Curry Dressing

Curry spices add an unexpected twist to this salad. The warm flavors combine especially well with the sweet shrimp and grated apple. Curry paste is needed here rather than curry powder, as there is no cooking, which is necessary for bringing out the flavors of powdered spices.

INGREDIENTS

Serves 4

1 ripe tomato

½ iceberg lettuce

1 small onion

1 small bunch fresh cilantro

1 tablespoon lemon juice

1 pound shelled, cooked shrimp

1 apple

8 whole shrimp, 8 lemon wedges and
    4 fresh cilantro sprigs, to garnish

salt

For the curry dressing

5 tablespoons mayonnaise

1 teaspoon mild curry paste

1 tablespoon ketchup

sake

1 To peel the tomato, cut a cross in the skin with a knife and immerse in boiling water for 30 seconds. Drain and cool under running water. Peel off the skin. Halve the tomato, push the seeds out with your thumb and discard them. Cut the flesh into large dice.

2 Finely shred the lettuce and put in a large bowl, then finely chop the onion and cilantro. Add to the bowl with the tomato, moisten with lemon juice and season with salt.

3 To make the dressing, combine the mayonnaise, curry paste and ketchup in a small bowl. Add 2 tablespoons water to thin the dressing and season to taste with salt.

COOK'S TIP

Fresh cilantro is inclined to wilt if it is kept out of water. Put it in a jar of water, cover with a plastic bag and place in the refrigerator, and it will stay fresh for several days.

---

4 Combine the shrimp with the dressing and stir gently so that all the shrimp are coated with the dressing.

5 Quarter and core the apple and grate into the shrimp and dressing mixture.

6 Distribute the shredded lettuce mixture among four serving plates or bowls. Pile the shrimp mixture in the center of each and decorate each with two whole shrimp, two lemon wedges and a sprig of cilantro.

Shrimp and Mint Salad

Fresh, uncooked shrimp make all the difference to this salad, and cooking them in butter adds to the flavor. Garnish with shavings of fresh coconut for a tropical topping, if desired.

INGREDIENTS

Serves 4

12 large fresh, uncooked shrimp
1 tablespoon unsalted butter
1 tablespoon Thai fish sauce
juice of 1 lime
3 tablespoons coconut milk
1 teaspoon sugar
1 garlic clove, crushed
1-inch piece fresh ginger, peeled
    and grated
2 red chiles, seeded and finely chopped
2 tablespoons fresh mint leaves
8 ounces light green lettuce leaves
ground black pepper

1 Carefully peel the uncooked shrimp, removing and discarding the heads and outer shells, but leaving the tails intact.

2 Using a sharp knife, carefully remove the dark-colored vein that runs along the back of each shrimp.

3 Melt the butter in a large frying pan. When the melted butter is foaming, add the shrimp and toss over high heat until they turn pink. Remove from the heat; it is important not to cook them for too long so that their tenderness is retained.

4 In a small bowl, combine the fish sauce, lime juice, coconut milk, sugar, garlic, ginger and chiles. Season to taste with freshly ground black pepper.

5 Toss the warm shrimp in the sauce with the mint leaves. Arrange the lettuce leaves on a serving plate and place the shrimp and mint mixture in the center.

VARIATION

Instead of shrimp, this dish works very well with lobster tails, if you are feeling very extravagant.

COOK'S TIP

If you can't find any fresh, uncooked shrimp you could use frozen ones. To make the most of their flavor, toss very quickly in the hot butter when they are completely thawed.

Mixed Seafood Salad

Use fresh seafood that is in season, or you can use a combination of fresh and frozen seafood.

INGREDIENTS

Serves 6–8

12 ounces small squid

1 small onion, cut into quarters

1 bay leaf

7 ounces uncooked shrimp, in
    their shells

1½ pounds fresh mussels, in their shells

1 pound fresh small clams

¾ cup white wine

1 fennel bulb

For the dressing

5 tablespoons extra-virgin olive oil

3 tablespoons lemon juice

1 garlic clove, finely chopped

salt and ground black pepper

1 Working near the sink, clean the squid by first peeling off the thin skin from the body section. Rinse well.

2 Pull the head and tentacles away from the sac section. Some of the intestines will come away with the head. Remove and discard the translucent quill and any remaining insides from the sac. Sever the tentacles and head.

3 Discard the head and intestines. Remove the small, hard beak from the base of the tentacles. Rinse the sac and tentacles under cold water. Drain.

4 Bring a large pan of water to a boil. Add the onion and bay leaf. Drop in the squid and cook for about 10 minutes or until tender. Remove with a slotted spoon and let cool before slicing into rings ½ inch wide. Cut each tentacle section into two pieces. Set aside.

5 Drop the shrimp into the same boiling water and cook for about 2 minutes, until they turn pink. Remove with a slotted spoon. Shell and devein. (The cooking liquid may be strained and kept for soup.)

6 Cut the "beards" from the mussels. Scrub and rinse the mussels and clams well in several changes of cold water. Place in a large saucepan with the wine. Cover and steam until all the shells have opened. (Discard any that do not open.) Lift the clams and mussels out of the pan.

7 Remove all the clams from their shells with a small spoon. Place in a large serving bowl. Remove all but eight of the mussels from their shells and add them to the clams in the bowl. Leave the remaining mussels in their half-shells, and set aside.

8 Cut the green, ferny part of the fennel off of the bulb. Chop finely and set aside. Chop the bulb into bite-sized pieces and add it to the serving bowl with the squid and shrimp.

9 To make the dressing, combine the oil, lemon juice and garlic in a bowl. Add the reserved chopped fennel green and salt and pepper to taste. Pour onto the salad, and toss well. Decorate with the remaining mussels in their half-shells. Serve at room temperature or lightly chilled.

Avocado, Crab and Cilantro Salad

The sweet richness of crab combines especially well with ripe avocado, fresh cilantro and tomato.

Serves 4

1½ pounds small new potatoes

1 fresh mint sprig

2 pounds boiled crabs or 10 ounces frozen
    crab meat

1 endive or Boston lettuce

6 ounces mache or baby
    spinach leaves

1 large ripe avocado, peeled and sliced

6 ounces cherry tomatoes

salt, ground black pepper and freshly
    grated nutmeg

For the dressing

5 tablespoons olive oil

1 tablespoon lime juice

3 tablespoons chopped fresh cilantro

½ teaspoon sugar

1 Scrape or peel the potatoes. Cover with water, add a good pinch of salt and a sprig of mint. Bring to a boil and simmer for about 15 minutes, until tender. Drain the potatoes, cover and keep warm until needed.

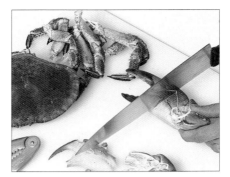

2 Remove the legs and claws from each crab. Crack these open with the back of a chopping knife, and remove the white meat.

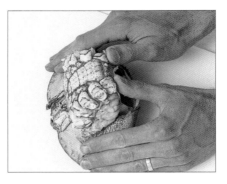

3 Turn the crab on its back and push the rear leg section away with the thumb and forefinger of each hand. Remove the flesh from inside the shell.

4 Discard the "dead men's fingers," the soft gills that the crab uses to filter impurities in its diet. Apart from these and the shell, everything else is edible, both white and dark meat.

5 Split the central body section open with a knife, and remove the white and dark flesh with a pick or skewer.

6 Combine all the dressing ingredients in a screw-top jar and shake. Put the salad leaves in a large bowl, pour on the dressing and toss well.

7 Distribute the leaves among four serving plates. Top with the avocado, crab, tomatoes and warm new potatoes. Season with salt, pepper and freshly grated nutmeg and serve.

COOK'S TIP

Young crabs offer the sweetest meat, but are more difficult to prepare than older, larger ones. The female crab carries more flesh than the male which is considered to have a better overall flavor. The male crab, shown here, is identified by his narrow apron flap at the rear. The female has a broad flap, under which she carries her eggs. Frozen crab meat is a good alternative to fresh and retains much of its original sweetness.

Thai Noodle Salad

The addition of coconut milk and sesame oil gives an unusual nutty flavor to the dressing for this colorful noodle salad.

INGREDIENTS

Serves 4–6

12 ounces ramen noodles

1 large carrot, cut into thin strips

1 bunch asparagus, trimmed and cut into 1½-inch lengths

1 red bell pepper, seeded and cut into fine strips

4 ounces snow peas, trimmed

4 ounces baby corn, halved lengthwise

4 ounces beansprouts

1 can (4 ounces) water chestnuts, drained and finely sliced

1 lime, cut into wedges, ½ cup roasted peanuts, roughly chopped, and fresh cilantro leaves, to garnish

For the dressing

3 tablespoons roughly torn fresh basil

5 tablespoons roughly chopped fresh mint

1 cup coconut milk

2 tablespoons dark sesame oil

1 tablespoon grated fresh ginger

2 garlic cloves, finely chopped

juice of 1 lime

2 scallions, finely chopped

salt and cayenne pepper

2 Cook the noodles in a saucepan of boiling water, following the directions on the package, until just tender. Drain, rinse under cold running water and drain again.

3 Cook all the vegetables, except the water chestnuts, in separate saucepans of boiling, lightly salted water, until they are tender but still crisp. Drain, plunge them immediately into cold water and drain again.

4 Toss the noodles, vegetables and dressing to combine. Arrange on individual serving plates and garnish with the lime wedges, chopped peanuts and cilantro leaves.

1 To make the dressing, combine all the ingredients in a bowl and mix well. Season to taste with salt and cayenne pepper.

Shrimp and Noodle Salad with Fragrant Herbs

A light, refreshing salad with all the tangy flavor of the sea. Instead of shrimp, you can also use squid, scallops, mussels or crab.

INGREDIENTS

Serves 4

4 ounces cellophane noodles, soaked in hot water until soft
16 shelled cooked shrimp
1 small green bell pepper, seeded and cut into strips
¹/₂ cucumber, cut into strips
1 tomato, cut into strips
2 shallots, finely sliced
salt and ground black pepper
fresh cilantro leaves, to garnish

For the dressing
1 tablespoon rice-wine vinegar
2 tablespoons Thai fish sauce
2 tablespoons lime juice
¹/₂ teaspoon grated fresh ginger
1 lemongrass stalk, finely chopped
1 red chile, seeded and finely sliced
2 tablespoons roughly chopped fresh mint
few sprigs of tarragon, roughly chopped
1 tablespoon snipped fresh chives
pinch of salt

1 To make the dressing, combine all the ingredients in a small bowl and whisk well.

2 Drain the noodles, then plunge them in a saucepan of boiling water for 1 minute. Drain, rinse under cold running water and drain again well.

3 In a large bowl, combine the noodles with the green pepper, cucumber, tomato and shallots. Lightly season with salt and pepper, then toss with the dressing.

> ### COOK'S TIP
>
> Shrimp are available ready-cooked and often shelled. To cook shrimp, boil them for 5 minutes. Let them cool in the cooking liquid, then gently pull off the tail shell and twist off the head.

4 Spoon the noodles onto individual serving plates, arranging the shrimp on top. Garnish with a few cilantro leaves and serve immediately.

Egg Noodle Salad with Sesame Chicken

Quickly stir-fried chicken is served warm in a nest of crisp salad vegetables and noodles.

INGREDIENTS

Serves 4–6

14 ounces fresh thin egg noodles

1 carrot, cut into long fine strips

2 ounces snow peas, trimmed, cut into fine strips and blanched

½ cup beansprouts, blanched

2 tablespoons olive oil

8 ounces skinless, boneless chicken breast, finely sliced

2 tablespoons sesame seeds, toasted

2 scallions, finely sliced diagonally, and fresh cilantro leaves, to garnish

For the dressing

3 tablespoons sherry vinegar

5 tablespoons soy sauce

4 tablespoons sesame oil

6 tablespoons light olive oil

1 garlic clove, finely chopped

1 teaspoon grated fresh ginger

salt and ground black pepper

1 To make the dressing, whisk all the ingredients in a small bowl. Season to taste.

2 Cook the noodles in a large saucepan of boiling water. Stir them occasionally to separate. They will take only a few minutes to cook; be careful not to overcook them. Drain the noodles, rinse under cold running water and drain well. Transfer into a bowl.

3 Add the carrot, snow peas and beansprouts to the noodles. Pour in about half the dressing, then toss the mixture well and adjust the seasoning according to taste.

4 Heat the oil in a large frying pan. Add the chicken and stir-fry for 3 minutes or until cooked and golden. Remove from the heat. Add the sesame seeds and drizzle on some of the remaining dressing.

5 Arrange the noodle mixture on individual serving plates, making a nest on each plate. Spoon the chicken on top. Sprinkle with the scallions and cilantro leaves and serve any remaining dressing separately.

Chicken and Pasta Salad

This is a delicious way to use up left-over cooked chicken and, with the pasta, it makes a filling meal.

INGREDIENTS

Serves 4

8 ounces tricolored pasta spirals

2 tablespoons pesto

1 tablespoon olive oil

1 tomato

12 pitted black olives

8 ounces green beans, cooked

12 ounces cooked chicken, cubed

salt and ground black pepper

fresh basil, to garnish

3 Peel the tomato by cutting a cross in the skin and plunging it in boiling water for about 30 seconds. The skin will now pull off easily. Cut the tomato into small cubes.

4 Add the tomato and olives to the pasta. Cut the green beans into 1½-inch lengths. Add the beans and chicken and season to taste. Toss gently, transfer to a serving platter, garnish with basil, and serve.

1 Cook the pasta in plenty of boiling, salted water until *al dente* (for about 12 minutes or as directed on the package).

2 Drain the pasta and rinse in plenty of cold running water. Put in a bowl and stir in the pesto and olive oil.

Chicken Salad with Garlic Bread

This makes a light first course for eight people or a substantial main course for four.

INGREDIENTS

Serves 4

4–4¹⁄₂ pounds chicken

1¹⁄₄ cups white wine and water, mixed

24 slices French bread, ¹⁄₄ inch thick

1 garlic clove, peeled

8 ounces green beans

4 ounces baby spinach

2 celery stalks, thinly sliced

2 sun-dried tomatoes, chopped

2 scallions, thinly sliced

fresh chives and parsley, to garnish

For the vinaigrette

2 tablespoons red wine vinegar

6 tablespoons olive oil

1 tablespoon whole-grain mustard

1 tablespoon honey

2 tablespoons chopped fresh mixed herbs,
    such as thyme, parsley, chives

2 teaspoons finely chopped capers

salt and ground black pepper

1 Preheat the oven to 375°F. Put the chicken into a casserole with the wine and water. Cook for 1¹⁄₂ hours, until tender. Let cool in the liquid. Discard the skin and bones and cut the flesh into small pieces.

2 To make the vinaigrette, put all the ingredients into a screw-top jar and shake vigorously to combine. Adjust the seasoning to taste if necessary.

3 Toast the French bread under the broiler or in the oven until dry and golden brown, then lightly rub with the peeled garlic clove.

4 Trim the green beans, cut into 2-inch lengths and cook in boiling water until just tender. Drain and rinse under cold running water.

5 Wash the spinach, discarding the stalks, and tear into small pieces. Arrange on individual serving plates with the celery, green beans, sun-dried tomatoes, chicken and scallions.

6 Spoon on the vinaigrette. Arrange the toasted slices of French bread on top, garnish with fresh chives and parsley and serve immediately.

Warm Chicken Salad

Succulent pieces of chicken are combined with vegetables and rice in a light chili dressing.

INGREDIENTS

Serves 6

2 ounces mixed salad leaves

2 ounces baby spinach leaves

2 ounces watercress

2 tablespoons chili sauce

2 tablespoons dry sherry

1 tablespoon soy sauce

1 tablespoon ketchup

2 teaspoons olive oil

8 shallots, finely chopped

1 garlic clove, crushed

12 ounces skinless, boneless chicken
  breast, cut into thin strips

1 red bell pepper, seeded and sliced

6 ounces snow peas, trimmed

1 can (14 ounces) baby corn, drained
  and halved

10 ounces brown rice, cooked

salt and ground black pepper

fresh parsley sprig, to garnish

1 If any of the mixed salad leaves
are large, tear them into
smaller pieces and arrange with
the spinach leaves on a serving
dish. Add the watercress and toss
to mix.

2 In a small bowl, combine the
chili sauce, sherry, soy sauce
and ketchup. Set the sauce
mixture aside.

3 Heat the oil in a large, non-
stick frying pan or wok. Add
the shallots and garlic and stir-fry
over medium heat for 1 minute.

4 Add the chicken to the pan
and stir-fry for another
3–4 minutes.

5 Add the pepper, snow peas,
baby corn and rice, and stir-
fry for another 2–3 minutes.

6 Pour in the chili sauce mixture
and stir-fry for
2–3 minutes, until hot and
bubbling. Season to taste.

7 Spoon the chicken mixture
onto the salad leaves, toss and
serve immediately, garnished with
a sprig of fresh parsley.

VARIATION

Use other lean meat such as turkey
breast, beef or pork in place of the
chicken.

Spicy Chicken Salad

Marinate the chicken in advance for this tasty salad, which is otherwise quick to prepare.

INGREDIENTS

Serves 6

1 teaspoon ground cumin seeds
1 teaspoon paprika
1 teaspoon ground turmeric
1–2 garlic cloves, crushed
2 tablespoons lime juice
4 chicken breasts, skinned and boned
8 ounces rigatoni
1 red bell pepper, seeded and chopped
2 celery stalks, thinly sliced
1 shallot or small onion, finely chopped
¼ cup stuffed green olives, halved
2 tablespoons honey
1 tablespoon whole-grain mustard
1–2 tablespoons lime juice
mixed salad leaves
salt and ground black pepper

2 Preheat the oven to 400°F. Put the chicken on a broiler pan in a single layer and bake for 20 minutes. (Alternatively, cook for 8–10 minutes on each side.)

3 Cook the rigatoni in a large pan of boiling, salted water until *al dente*. Drain and rinse under cold water. Let drain thoroughly.

4 Put the red pepper, celery, shallot or small onion and olives into a large bowl with the pasta. Combine.

5 Combine the honey, mustard and lime juice in a small bowl and pour it over the pasta mixture. Toss to coat.

6 Cut the chicken breasts into bite-sized pieces. Arrange the mixed salad leaves on a serving dish, spoon the pasta mixture into the center and top with the spicy chicken pieces.

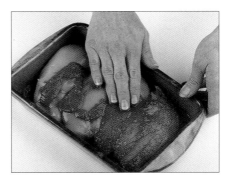

1 Mix the cumin, paprika, turmeric, garlic and lime juice in a bowl. Season with salt and pepper. Rub this mixture onto the chicken breasts. Lay these in a shallow dish, cover with plastic wrap and set in a cool place for about 3 hours or overnight.

Chicken Maryland Salad

Grilled chicken, corn, bacon, banana and watercress combine in a sensational main-course salad. Serve with baked potatoes topped with a pat of butter.

Serves 4

4 boneless chicken breasts

oil, for brushing

8 ounces bacon

4 ears of corn

3 tablespoons butter (optional)

4 ripe bananas, peeled and halved

4 firm tomatoes, halved

1 escarole or Boston lettuce

1 bunch watercress

salt and ground black pepper

For the dressing

5 tablespoons peanut oil

1 tablespoon white wine vinegar

2 teaspoons maple syrup

2 teaspoons prepared mild mustard

1 Season the chicken breasts, brush with oil and grill for 15 minutes, turning once. Grill the bacon for 8–10 minutes or until crisp.

2 Bring a large saucepan of salted water to a boil. Shuck and trim the corn or leave the husks on if you prefer. Boil for 20 minutes.

3 For extra flavor, brush the corn with butter and brown on the grill. Grill the bananas and tomatoes for 6–8 minutes; you can brush these with butter too if desired.

4 To make the dressing, combine the oil, vinegar, maple syrup and mustard with 1 tablespoon water in a screw-top jar and shake well.

5 Wash the lettuce and watercress leaves and spin dry. Put into a large bowl, pour on the dressing and toss well.

6 Distribute the salad leaves among four large serving plates. Slice the chicken and arrange over the salad leaves with the bacon, banana, corn and tomatoes.

Chicken, Tongue and Gruyère Salad

The rich, sweet flavors of this salad marry well with the tart, peppery watercress. A minted lemon dressing freshens the overall effect. Serve with warm new potatoes.

INGREDIENTS

Serves 4

2 chicken breasts, skinned
    and boned
½ chicken bouillon cube
8 ounces tongue or ham, sliced
    ¼-inch thick
8 ounces Gruyère cheese
1 lollo rosso lettuce
1 endive
1 bunch watercress
2 green apples, cored and sliced
3 celery stalks, sliced
4 tablespoons sesame seeds, toasted
salt, ground black pepper and freshly
    grated nutmeg

For the dressing
5 tablespoons peanut or sunflower oil
1 teaspoon sesame oil
3 tablespoons lemon juice
2 teaspoons chopped fresh mint
3 drops Tabasco sauce

1 Place the chicken breasts in a shallow saucepan, cover with 1¼ cups water, add the ½ bouillon cube and bring to a boil. Put the lid on the pan and simmer for 15 minutes. Drain, reserving the stock for another occasion, then cool the chicken under cold running water.

2 To make the dressing, measure the oils, lemon juice, mint and Tabasco sauce into a screw-top jar and shake well. Cut the chicken, tongue or ham and cheese into fine strips. Moisten with a little dressing and set aside.

3 Combine the lettuce and watercress leaves with the apple and celery. Add the dressing and toss. Distribute among four large serving plates. Pile the chicken, tongue or ham and cheese in the center, sprinkle on sesame seeds, season with salt, pepper and freshly grated nutmeg and serve.

Curried Chicken Salad

A smooth, mildly spicy sauce with the distinctive tang of fresh cilantro blends well with lean chicken on a bed of pasta and vegetables.

INGREDIENTS

Serves 4

2 cooked chicken breasts, skinned and boned

6 ounces green beans

12 ounces multi-colored penne

⅔ cup plain yogurt

1 teaspoon mild curry powder

1 garlic clove, crushed

1 green chile, seeded and finely chopped

2 tablespoons chopped fresh cilantro

4 firm ripe tomatoes, skinned, seeded and cut in strips

salt and ground black pepper

fresh cilantro leaves, to garnish

1 Cut the chicken into strips. Cut the beans into 1-inch lengths and cook in boiling water for 5 minutes. Drain and rinse under cold water.

2 Cook the pasta in a large pan of boiling, salted water until *al dente*. Drain and rinse thoroughly.

3 To make the sauce, combine the yogurt, curry powder, garlic, chile and chopped cilantro in a bowl. Stir in the chicken pieces and let stand for 30 minutes.

4 Transfer the pasta to a large serving bowl and toss with the beans and tomatoes. Spoon this over the chicken and sauce mixture. Garnish with the cilantro and serve.

"Poor Boy" Steak Salad

"Poor Boys" started life in the Italian Creole community of New Orleans when the poor survived on sandwiches filled with leftover scraps. Times have improved since then, and today the "Poor Boy" sandwich is commonly filled with tender beef and other goodies. This is a salad version of a Poor Boy.

INGREDIENTS

Serves 4

4 sirloin or rump steaks, each about
   6 ounces
1 escarole lettuce
1 bunch watercress
4 tomatoes, quartered
4 large gherkins, sliced
4 scallions, sliced
4 canned artichoke hearts, halved
6 ounces button mushrooms, sliced
12 green olives
½ cup French Dressing
salt and ground black pepper

1 Season the steaks with black pepper. Cook over a medium grill for 6–8 minutes, turning once, until medium-rare. Cover and let rest in a warm place.

2 Combine the lettuce and watercress leaves with the tomatoes, gherkins, scallions, artichoke hearts, mushrooms and olives and toss with the French Dressing.

3 Divide the salad among four serving plates. Slice each steak diagonally and arrange on the salad. Season with salt and serve immediately.

Waldorf Salad

Waldorf Salad first appeared at the Waldorf-Astoria Hotel, in New York in the 1890s. Originally it consisted of apples, celery and mayonnaise, and was commonly served with duck, ham and goose. This modern-day version often includes meat and is something of a meal in itself.

INGREDIENTS

Serves 4

3 apples

1 tablespoon lemon juice

2 slices cooked ham, each about 6 ounces

2 celery stalks

$^2/_3$ cup mayonnaise

1 escarole lettuce or endive

1 small radicchio, finely shredded

$^1/_2$ bunch watercress

3 tablespoons walnut or olive oil

$^1/_2$ cup broken walnuts, toasted

salt and ground black pepper

1 Peel, core, slice and finely shred the apples. Moisten with lemon juice to keep them white. Cut the ham into 2-inch strips. Cut the celery stalks into similar-sized pieces. Combine the apples, ham and celery in a bowl.

2 Add the mayonnaise and mix thoroughly.

3 Shred all the salad leaves finely, then moisten with oil. Distribute the leaves among four serving plates. Pile the mayonnaise mixture in the center, sprinkle on toasted walnuts, season and serve.

Chicken Liver, Bacon and Tomato Salad

Warm salads are especially welcome during the autumn months when the days are growing shorter and cooler. This rich salad includes sweet spinach and the bitter leaves of frisée lettuce.

INGREDIENTS

Serves 4

8 ounces baby spinach, stems removed

1 frisée lettuce

7 tablespoons peanut or sunflower oil

6 ounces bacon, cut into strips

3 ounces day-old bread, crusts removed and cut into short fingers

1 pound chicken livers

4 ounces cherry tomatoes

salt and ground black pepper

1 Place the spinach and lettuce leaves in a salad bowl. Heat 4 tablespoons of the oil in a large frying pan, add the bacon and cook for 3–4 minutes or until crisp and brown. Remove the bacon with a slotted spoon and drain on paper towels.

2 To make croûtons, fry the bread in the bacon-flavored oil, tossing until crisp and golden. Drain on paper towels.

3 Heat the remaining 3 tablespoons oil in the frying pan, add the chicken livers and fry briskly for 2–3 minutes. Place the chicken livers on the salad leaves and add the bacon, croûtons and tomatoes. Season, toss and serve warm.

VARIATION

If you can't find any baby spinach leaves you can use mache. Watercress would make a deliciously peppery substitute, but you should use less of it and bulk the salad out with a milder leaf so the watercress doesn't overwhelm the other flavors.

Curry Fried Pork and Rice Vermicelli Salad

Pork adds a delicious taste to this popular salad.

INGREDIENTS

Serves 4

8 ounces lean pork

2 garlic cloves, finely chopped

2½-inch slices fresh ginger, peeled and finely chopped

2–3 tablespoons rice wine

3 tablespoons vegetable oil

2 lemongrass stalks, finely chopped

2 teaspoons curry powder

¾ cup beansprouts

8 ounces rice vermicelli, soaked in warm water until soft, then drained

½ lettuce, finely shredded

2 tablespoons fresh mint leaves

lemon juice and Thai fish sauce, to taste

salt and ground black pepper

2 scallions, chopped, ¼ cup toasted peanuts, chopped, and pork cracklings (optional) to garnish

1 Cut the pork into thin strips. Place in a shallow dish with half the garlic and ginger. Season with salt and pepper, pour on 2 tablespoons rice wine and marinate for at least 1 hour.

2 Heat the oil in a frying pan. Add the remaining garlic and ginger and fry for a few seconds until fragrant and golden. Stir in the strips of pork, with the marinade, and add the lemongrass and curry powder.

3 Fry over high heat until the pork is golden and cooked through, adding more rice wine if the mixture seems too dry.

4 Place the beansprouts in a sieve. Blanch them by lowering the sieve into a saucepan of boiling water for 1 minute, then drain and refresh under cold running water. Drain again. Using the same water, cook the rice vermicelli for 3–5 minutes, until tender. Drain and rinse under cold running water.

5 Drain the vermicelli well and transfer into a large bowl. Add the beansprouts, shredded lettuce and mint leaves. Season with lemon juice and fish sauce to taste. Toss lightly to combine the flavors.

6 Divide the vermicelli mixture among individual serving plates, making a nest on each plate. Arrange the pork mixture on top. Garnish with scallions, toasted peanuts and pork cracklings, if using. Serve. immediately.

Sweet Potato, Egg, Pork and Beet Salad

This dish is a delicious way to use up leftover roast pork. Sweet flavors balance well with the bitterness of the chicory leaves.

Serve 4

2 pounds sweet potatoes

4 heads chicory

5 eggs, hard-boiled

1 pound pickled beets

6 ounces cold roast pork

salt

For the dressing

5 tablespoons peanut or sunflower oil

2 tablespoons white wine vinegar

2 teaspoon Dijon mustard

1 teaspoon fennel seeds, crushed

1 Peel the sweet potatoes and dice into equal-sized pieces.

2 Add the diced sweet potatoes to a pan of boiling salted water. Bring back to a boil, then simmer for 10–15 minutes or until the potatoes are soft. Drain and let cool.

3 To make the dressing, combine the oil, vinegar, mustard and fennel seeds in a screw-top jar and shake.

4 Separate the chicory leaves and arrange them around the edge of four serving plates.

5 Pour two-thirds of the dressing over the sweet potatoes, stir in so that all the pieces of potato are coated in the dressing, and spoon on top of the chicory leaves.

6 Shell the hard-boiled eggs. Slice the eggs and beets, and arrange to make an attractive circle around the sweet potato.

7 Slice the pork, then cut into strips of around 1½ inches. Place in a bowl and moisten with the rest of the dressing.

8 Pile the strips of pork into the center of each salad. Season with salt and serve.

COOK'S TIP

To crush the fennel seeds, grind using a mortar and pestle. If you don't have this, use two spoons instead. For extra flavor, try toasting the fennel seeds before crushing.

Frankfurter Salad with Mustard Dressing

This is a last-minute salad, which you can throw together using mostly ingredients you have on hand.

INGREDIENTS

Serves 4

1½ pounds small new potatoes, scrubbed
    or scraped

2 eggs

12 ounces frankfurters

1 Boston lettuce

8 ounces baby spinach,
    stems removed

salt and ground black pepper

For the dressing

3 tablespoons safflower oil

2 tablespoons olive oil

1 tablespoon white wine vinegar

2 teaspoons mustard

1 teaspoon caraway seeds, crushed

2 Score the frankfurter skins cork-screw fashion with a small knife, then cover with boiling water and simmer for about 5 minutes to heat through. Drain well, cover and keep warm.

5 Moisten the warm potatoes and frankfurters with the remainder of the dressing and sprinkle on the salad.

3 To make the dressing, place all the ingredients in a screw-top jar and shake.

6 Finish the salad with sections of hard-boiled egg, season and serve warm.

1 Bring the potatoes to a boil in salted water and simmer for about 15 minutes or until tender. Drain, cover and keep warm. Hard-boil the eggs for 12 minutes. Refresh in cold water, shell and cut into quarters.

4 Moisten the salad leaves with half of the dressing and distribute among four large serving plates.

COOK'S TIP

This salad has a German taste to it and calls for a sweet-and-sour German-style mustard.

Bacon and Green Bean Pasta Salad

A tasty pasta salad, subtly flavored with bacon and tossed in a light, flavorful dressing.

INGREDIENTS

Serves 4

12 ounces whole-wheat pasta spirals
8 ounces green beans
8 strips bacon
12 ounces cherry tomatoes, halved
2 bunches scallions, chopped
1 can (14 ounces) chickpeas, drained

For the dressing

6 tablespoons tomato juice
2 tablespoons balsamic vinegar
1 teaspoon ground cumin
1 teaspoon ground coriander
2 tablespoons chopped fresh cilantro
salt and ground black pepper

2 Preheat the broiler and cook the bacon for 2–3 minutes on each side, until cooked. Dice the bacon and add to the beans.

3 Put the tomatoes, scallions and chickpeas in a large bowl. In a small bowl, combine the tomato juice, vinegar, spices, fresh cilantro and seasoning.

4 Pour the dressing into a large bowl. Drain the cooked pasta thoroughly and add to the tomato mixture with the green beans and bacon. Toss all the ingredients to mix thoroughly. Serve warm or cold.

1 Cook the pasta in a large saucepan of lightly salted, boiling water until *al dente*. Meanwhile, trim and halve the green beans and cook them in boiling water for about 5 minutes, until tender. Drain thoroughly and keep warm.

COOK'S TIP

Always rinse canned beans and pulses well before using, to remove as much of the brine (salt water) as possible.

Warm Pasta Salad with Asparagus

This warm salad is served with ham, eggs and Parmesan. A mustard dressing made from the thick part of the asparagus stalks provides a rich accompaniment.

INGREDIENTS

Serves 4

1 pound asparagus

1 pound dried tagliatelle

8 ounces cooked ham, sliced ¼-inch thick, and cut into fingers

2 eggs, hard-boiled and sliced

2 ounces piece Parmesan cheese

For the dressing

2 ounces cooked potato

5 tablespoons olive oil

1 tablespoon lemon juice

2 teaspoons Dijon mustard

½ cup vegetable stock

salt and ground black pepper

1 Bring a saucepan of salted water to the boil. Trim and discard the tough, woody part of the asparagus stalks. Cut the asparagus in half and boil the thicker halves for 12 minutes, adding the asparagus tips after 6 minutes. Refresh under cold water until warm, then drain.

2 Finely chop 5 ounces of the thicker asparagus pieces. Place in a food processor together with the dressing ingredients and process until smooth. Season the dressing to taste.

3 Boil the pasta in a large saucepan of salted water until *al dente*. Refresh under cold water.

4 Dress with the asparagus sauce and turn out into four pasta bowls. Top each pile of pasta with the some of the ham, eggs and asparagus tips. Finish with shavings of Parmesan cheese and serve warm.

Deviled Ham and Pineapple Salad

This tasty salad, with a crunchy topping of toasted almonds, can be quickly prepared using items from the pantry.

Serves 4

8 ounces whole-wheat penne

²/₃ cup plain yogurt

1 tablespoon cider vinegar

1 teaspoon whole-grain mustard

large pinch of sugar

2 tablespoons hot mango chutney

4 ounces cooked lean ham, cubed

1 can (7 ounces) pineapple chunks, drained

2 celery stalks, chopped

¹/₂ green bell pepper, seeded and diced

1 tablespoon toasted sliced almonds,
    chopped roughly

salt and ground black pepper

crusty bread, to serve

1 Cook the pasta in a large pan of salted boiling water until *al dente*. Drain and rinse thoroughly. Let cool.

2 To make the dressing, combine the yogurt, vinegar, mustard, sugar and mango chutney. Season with salt and pepper. Add the pasta and toss lightly.

3 Transfer the pasta to a serving dish. Add the ham, pineapple, celery and green pepper.

4 Sprinkle toasted almonds on top of the salad. Serve with crusty bread.

Pear and Pecan Nut Salad

Toasted pecans have a special affinity with crisp white pears. Their robust flavors combine well with a rich Blue Cheese and Chive Dressing to make this a salad to remember.

INGREDIENTS

Serves 4

½ cup shelled pecan nuts, roughly chopped

3 crisp pears

6 ounces young spinach, stems removed

1 escarole or Boston lettuce

1 radicchio

2 tablespoons Blue Cheese and Chive Dressing

salt and ground black pepper

crusty bread, to serve

1 Toast the pecan nuts under a moderate broiler to bring out their flavor.

COOK'S TIP

The pecan nuts will burn very quickly under the broiler, so keep constant watch over them and remove them as soon as they change color.

2 Cut the pears into even slices, leaving the skins intact but discarding the cores.

3 Place the spinach, lettuce and radicchio leaves into a large bowl. Add the pears and toasted pecans, pour over the Blue Cheese and Chive Dressing and toss well. Distribute among four large serving plates and season with salt and pepper. Serve the salad with warm crusty bread.

Goat Cheese and Fig Salad

*Fresh figs and walnuts are perfect
partners for goat cheese and toasted
buckwheat. The olive and nut oil
dressing contains no vinegar,
depending instead on the acidity of
the goat cheese.*

INGREDIENTS

Serves 4

1 cup couscous

2 tablespoons toasted buckwheat

1 egg, hard-boiled

2 tablespoons chopped fresh parsley

4 tablespoons olive oil

3 tablespoons walnut oil

4 ounces arugula leaves

½ frisée lettuce

6 ounces crumbly white goat cheese

½ cup broken walnuts, toasted

4 ripe figs, trimmed and cut into fourths
   (leave the pieces joined at the base)

1 Place the couscous and toasted
buckwheat in a bowl, cover
with boiling water and let soak for
15 minutes. Place in a sieve to
drain off any remaining water,
then spread out on a baking sheet
and let cool.

3 Toss the grated egg, parsley,
couscous and buckwheat in a
bowl. Combine the olive and
walnut oils, using half to moisten
the couscous mixture.

2 Shell the hard-boiled egg and
grate finely.

4 Toss the salad leaves in the
remaining oil and distribute
among four large serving plates.

5 Pile the couscous mixture in
the center of each plate, and
crumble the goat cheese on
top. Sprinkle with toasted walnuts,
place a fig in the center of each
plate and serve.

COOK'S TIP

Goat cheeses vary in strength
from the youngest, which are
soft and mild, to strongly-
flavored, aged cheeses, which
have a firm and crumbly texture.
The crumbly varieties are best
suited to salads.

Avocado, Tomato and Mozzarella Salad

This popular salad is made from ingredients representing the colors of the Italian flag—a sunny, cheerful dish! The addition of pasta turns it into a main course meal for a light lunch.

INGREDIENTS

Serves 4

6 ounces pasta bows (farfalle)
6 ripe red tomatoes
8 ounces mozzarella cheese
1 large ripe avocado
2 tablespoons chopped fresh basil
2 tablespoons pine nuts, toasted
fresh basil sprig, to garnish

For the dressing
6 tablespoons olive oil
2 tablespoons wine vinegar
1 teaspoon balsamic vinegar (optional)
1 teaspoon whole-grain mustard
pinch of sugar
salt and ground black pepper

1 Cook the pasta bows in plenty of salted, boiling water until *al dente*.

2 Slice the tomatoes and mozzarella cheese into thin rounds.

3 Halve the avocado, remove the pit and peel off the skin. Slice the flesh lengthwise.

4 Whisk the dressing ingredients together in a small bowl.

5 Arrange the tomato, mozzarella and avocado slices in overlapping slices around the edge of a flat serving plate.

6 Toss the pasta with half of the dressing and the chopped basil. Pile into the centre of the plate. Pour on the remaining dressing, sprinkle on the pine nuts and garnish with a sprig of fresh basil. Serve immediately.

COOK'S TIP

The pale green flesh of the avocado quickly discolors once it is cut. Prepare it at the last minute and place immediately in dressing. If you do have to prepare it ahead, squeeze lemon juice over the cut side and cover with plastic wrap.

Roquefort and Walnut Pasta Salad

This is a simple, earthy salad, relying totally on the quality of the ingredients. There is no real substitute for the Roquefort—a blue-veined ewe's-milk cheese from southwestern France.

Serves 4

8 ounces pasta shapes

selection of salad leaves such as arugula, curly endive, mache, baby spinach, and radicchio

2 tablespoons walnut oil

4 tablespoons sunflower oil

2 tablespoons red wine vinegar or sherry vinegar

8 ounces Roquefort cheese, roughly crumbled

1 cup walnut halves

salt and ground black pepper

3 Pile the pasta in the center of the salad leaves, sprinkle on the crumbled Roquefort and pour on the dressing.

4 Sprinkle the walnuts on top. Toss the salad just before serving.

1 Cook the pasta in plenty of salted, boiling water until *al dente*. Drain well and cool. Place the salad leaves in a bowl.

2 Whisk together the walnut oil, sunflower oil and vinegar. Season with salt and pepper to taste.

COOK'S TIP

Toast the walnuts to add extra flavor.

Pasta, Asparagus and Potato Salad

Made with whole-wheat pasta, this delicious salad is a real treat, especially when made with fresh asparagus just in season.

INGREDIENTS

Serves 4

8 ounces whole-wheat pasta shapes

4 tablespoons extra-virgin olive oil

12 ounces baby new potatoes

8 ounces asparagus

4 ounces piece Parmesan cheese

salt and ground black pepper

1 Cook the pasta in salted, boiling water until *al dente*.

2 Drain well and toss with the olive oil while the pasta is still warm. Season with salt and ground black pepper.

3 Scrub the potatoes and cook in boiling salted water for about 15 minutes, or until tender. Drain the potatoes and toss together with the pasta.

4 Trim any woody ends off the asparagus and halve the stalks if very long. Blanch in boiling salted water for 6 minutes, until bright green and still crunchy. Drain. Plunge into cold water to stop the asparagus cooking and allow to cool. Drain and dry on kitchen paper.

5 Toss the asparagus with the potatoes and pasta, adjust the seasoning to taste and transfer to a shallow serving bowl. Using a vegetable peeler, shave the Parmesan over the salad.

Zucchini, Carrots and Pecan Salad

Chunks of warm fried zucchini are served with a crisp tangy salad in pockets of pita bread.

INGREDIENTS

Serves 2

2 carrots

¼ cup pecans

4 scallions , sliced

¼ cup plain yogurt

7 teaspoons olive oil

1 teaspoon lemon juice

1 tablespoon chopped fresh mint

2 zucchini

¼ cup flour

2 pita breads

salt and ground black pepper

shredded lettuce, to serve

3 In a clean bowl, make the dressing. Whisk the yogurt with 1½ teaspoons of the olive oil, the lemon juice and the mint. Stir the dressing into the carrot mixture and mix well. Cover and chill until required.

5 Heat the remaining oil in a large frying pan. Add the coated zucchini slices and cook for 3–4 minutes, turning once, until browned. Drain the zucchini on paper towels.

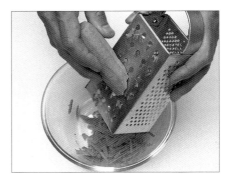

1 Trim and peel the carrots. Grate them coarsely into a bowl.

4 Trim the zucchini. Cut them diagonally into slices. Season the flour with salt and pepper. Spread it out on a plate and turn the zucchini slices in it until they are well coated.

6 Make a slit in each pita bread to form a pocket. Fill the pitas with the carrot mixture and the zucchini slices. Serve on a bed of shredded lettuce.

2 Stir in the pecans and scallions and toss well.

COOK'S TIP

Warm the pita bread in the oven or under a medium broiler. Do not fill the pita breads too soon or the carrot mixture will make the bread soggy.

Pasta, Olive and Avocado Salad

The ingredients of this salad are united by a wonderful sun-dried tomato and fresh basil dressing.

INGREDIENTS

Serves 6

8 ounces pasta spirals or other small
    pasta shapes
1 can (4 ounces) corn, drained, or frozen
    corn, thawed
$\frac{1}{2}$ red bell pepper, seeded and diced
8 black olives, pitted and sliced
3 scallions , finely chopped
2 medium avocados

For the dressing
2 sun-dried tomato halves, loose-packed
    (not preserved in oil)
$1\frac{1}{2}$ tablespoons balsamic or white
    wine vinegar
$1\frac{1}{2}$ tablespoons red wine vinegar
$\frac{1}{2}$ garlic clove, crushed
$\frac{1}{2}$ teaspoon salt
5 tablespoons olive oil
1 tablespoon chopped fresh basil

1 To make the dressing, drop the sun-dried tomatoes into a pan containing 1-inch boiling water and simmer for about 3 minutes, until tender. Drain and chop finely.

2 Combine the sun-dried tomatoes, both vinegars, garlic and salt in a food processor. With the machine on, add the olive oil in a stream. Stir in the basil.

3 Cook the pasta in a large pan of salted boiling water until *al dente*. Drain well. In a large bowl, combine the pasta, corn, red pepper, olives and scallions. Add the dressing and toss well.

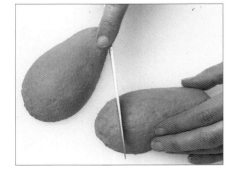

4 Just before serving, peel and pit the avocados and cut the flesh into cubes. Mix gently into the pasta, then place the salad on a serving dish. Serve at room temperature.

Roasted Pepper and Mushroom Pasta Salad

A combination of grilled peppers and two different kinds of mushroom makes this salad colorful as well as nutritious.

INGREDIENTS

Serves 6

1 red bell pepper, halved

1 yellow bell pepper, halved

1 green bell pepper, halved

12 ounces whole-wheat pasta shells or twists

2 tablespoons olive oil

3 tablespoons balsamic vinegar

5 tablespoons tomato juice

2 tablespoons chopped fresh basil

1 tablespoon chopped fresh thyme

$2\frac{1}{4}$ cups shiitake mushrooms, diced

$2\frac{1}{4}$ cups oyster mushrooms, sliced

14-ounce can black-eyed peas, drained and rinsed

$\frac{3}{4}$ cup golden raisins

2 bunches scallions , finely chopped

salt and ground black pepper

1 Preheat the grill to hot. Put the peppers cut-side down on a grill pan rack and place under the grill for 10–15 minutes, until the skins are charred. Cover the peppers with a clean, damp tea towel and set aside to cool.

2 Meanwhile, cook the pasta shells or twists in lightly salted, boiling water until *al dente*, then drain thoroughly.

3 Mix together the oil, vinegar, tomato juice, basil and thyme, add to the warm pasta and toss.

4 Remove and discard the skins from the peppers. Seed and slice and add to the pasta.

5 Add the mushrooms, peas, golden raisins, scallions and seasoning. Toss the ingredients to mix and serve immediately. Alternatively, cover and chill in the refrigerator before serving.

Mediterranean Pasta Salad

A type of Salade Niçoise with pasta, conjuring up all the sunny flavors of the Mediterranean.

INGREDIENTS

Serves 4

8 ounces pasta shapes

6 ounces green beans

2 large ripe tomatoes

2 ounces fresh basil leaves

1 can (7 ounces) tuna fish in oil, drained

2 hard-boiled eggs, shelled and sliced
  or quartered

1 can (2 ounces) anchovy fillets, drained

capers and black olives, to taste

For the dressing

6 tablespoons extra-virgin olive oil

2 tablespoons white wine vinegar or
  lemon juice

2 garlic cloves, crushed

1/2 teaspoon Dijon mustard

2 tablespoons chopped fresh basil

salt and ground black pepper

1 To make the dressing, whisk all
  the ingredients in a small bowl.
Set aside to infuse while you
prepare the salad.

COOK'S TIP

Don't be tempted to chill this
salad—the flavor
will be dulled.

2 Cook the pasta in plenty of
  salted, boiling water until *al
dente*. Drain well and cool.

3 Trim the green beans and
  blanch in salted, boiling water
for 3 minutes. Drain and refresh in
cold water.

4 Slice the tomatoes and arrange
  on the bottom of a serving
bowl. Moisten with a little dressing
and cover with a quarter of the
basil leaves. Then cover with the
beans. Moisten with a little more
dressing and cover with a third of
the remaining basil.

5 Cover the vegetables with the
  pasta tossed in a little more
dressing, half the remaining basil
and the roughly flaked tuna.

6 Arrange the eggs on top, then
  finally sprinkle on the
anchovy fillets, capers and olives.
Spoon on the remaining dressing
and garnish with the remaining
basil. Serve immediately.

Special Occasion Salads

~

Gado Gado

This classic Indonesian vegetable salad is served with a delicious hot peanut sauce.

INGREDIENTS

Serves 4–6

2 medium potatoes
6 ounces green beans, trimmed
6 ounces Chinese cabbage, shredded
1 iceberg lettuce
6 ounces beansprouts
½ cucumber, cut into fingers
5 ounces daikon radish, shredded
3 scallions
8 ounces firm tofu, cut into large slices
3 hard-boiled eggs, shelled and quartered
1 small bunch fresh cilantro
shrimp crackers, to serve

For the peanut sauce

1¼ cups raw peanuts
1 tablespoon vegetable oil
2 shallots or 1 small onion, finely chopped
1 garlic clove, crushed
1–2 small chiles, seeded and finely
   chopped
½-inch square shrimp paste or
   1 tablespoon Thai fish sauce (optional)
2 tablespoons tamarind sauce
½ cup coconut milk
1 tablespoon honey

1 Peel the potatoes. Bring to a boil in salted water and simmer for about 15 minutes or until tender. Cook the green beans for 3–4 minutes. Drain the potatoes and beans and refresh under cold running water.

2 To make the peanut sauce, dry-fry the peanuts in a wok, or place under a medium broiler, tossing them often to prevent burning.

3 Transfer the peanuts to a clean cloth and rub them vigorously with your hands to remove the papery skins. Place the peanuts in a food processor and blend for 2 minutes, until finely crushed.

4 Heat the vegetable oil in a wok and soften the shallots or onion, garlic and chiles without letting them color. Add the shrimp paste or fish sauce, if using, together with the tamarind sauce, coconut milk and honey.

5 Simmer briefly, add to the blended peanuts and process to form a thick sauce. Transfer to a small serving bowl and keep hot.

6 Arrange the potatoes, green beans and all the other salad ingredients on a large serving platter. Serve with the bowl of peanut sauce and shrimp crackers.

Composed Salads

Composed salads make perfect appetizers. They are light and colorful and lend themselves to endless variation—and the components can often be prepared ahead for quick assembly.

The French are masters of the composed salad. Any combination of ingredients can be used—let your imagination and your palate guide you. Arranged attractively on a plate or in a bowl, this type of salad offers contrasting flavors, textures and colors. Raw or cooked vegetables, fresh fruit, hard-boiled hen's or quail's eggs, smoked or cooked poultry, meat, fish or shellfish can all be used, but it is important that the dressing or other seasoning unites all the elements harmoniously.

Unlike a tossed salad such as Salade de Mesclun, in which the leaves are tossed with a simple vinaigrette, the components of a composed salad are kept more separate. The ingredients might be arranged in groups, sometimes on a base of lettuce or other leaves, or simply arranged in circles on the plate. Composed salads, like the famous Salade Niçoise or any of the following salads, are often served as a first course or a light main course, especially in warm weather. A tossed green salad is frequently eaten after the main course and is generally thought to cleanse the palate in preparation for the cheese course or dessert.

SHRIMP, AVOCADO AND CITRUS SALAD

INGREDIENTS

Serves 6

1 tablespoon lemon juice
1 tablespoon lime juice
1 tablespoon honey
3 tablespoons olive oil
2–3 tablespoons walnut oil
2 tablespoons snipped fresh chives
1 pound large cooked shrimp, shelled and deveined
1 avocado, peeled, pitted and cut into small dice
1 pink grapefruit, peeled and segmented
1 large navel orange, peeled and segmented
2 tablespoons pine nuts, toasted (optional)
salt and ground black pepper

1 Blend the lemon and lime juices, salt and pepper and honey in a small bowl. Slowly whisk in the olive oil, then the walnut oil, to make a creamy dressing. Stir in the chives.

2 Arrange the shrimp with the diced avocado and grapefruit and orange segments on individual serving plates. Drizzle on the dressing, sprinkle with the toasted pine nuts, if using, and serve.

SMOKED SALMON SALAD WITH DILL

INGREDIENTS

Serves 4

8 ounces smoked salmon, thinly sliced
1 fennel bulb, thinly sliced
1 medium cucumber, seeded and cut into julienne strips
2 tablespoons lemon juice
½ cup extra-virgin olive oil
2 tablespoons chopped fresh dill, plus a few sprigs to garnish
ground black pepper
caviar, to garnish (optional)

1 Arrange the smoked salmon slices on four individual serving plates and arrange the slices of fennel alongside, together with the cucumber strips.

2 Combine the lemon juice and pepper in a small bowl. Slowly whisk in the olive oil to make a creamy vinaigrette. Stir in the chopped dill.

3 Spoon a little vinaigrette on the fennel and cucumber. Drizzle the remaining vinaigrette on the smoked salmon and garnish with sprigs of dill. Top each salad with a spoonful of caviar, if desired, before serving.

CHICORY SALAD WITH ROQUEFORT

INGREDIENTS

Serves 4

2 tablespoons red wine vinegar
1 teaspoon Dijon mustard
¼ cup walnut oil
1–2 tablespoons sunflower oil
2 white or red heads chicory
1 celery heart or 4 celery stalks, cut into julienne strips
¾ cup walnut halves, lightly toasted
4 ounces Roquefort cheese
salt and ground black pepper
fresh parsley sprigs, to garnish

1 Whisk together the vinegar, mustard and salt and pepper to taste in a small bowl. Slowly whisk in the oils to make a vinaigrette.

2 Arrange the chicory on individual serving plates. Sprinkle on the celery and walnut halves. Crumble the Roquefort cheese on top of each salad, drizzle on a little vinaigrette and serve garnished with parsley sprigs.

Clockwise from far right: Shrimp, Avocado and Citrus Salad; Smoked Salmon Salad with Dill; and Chicory Salad with Roquefort.

Thai Fish Salad

For a tropical taste of the Far East, try this delicious fish salad scented with coconut, exotic fruit and warm Thai spices.

Serves 4

12 ounces fillet of red mullet
  or snapper
1 Romaine lettuce
½ lollo biondo lettuce
1 papaya or mango, peeled and sliced
1 large ripe tomato, cut into wedges
½ cucumber, peeled and cut into strips
3 scallions, sliced

For the marinade

1 teaspoon coriander seeds
1 teaspoon fennel seeds
½ teaspoon cumin seeds
1 teaspoon sugar
½ teaspoon hot chili sauce
2 tablespoons garlic oil
salt

For the dressing

1 tablespoon coconut milk
4 tablespoons peanut or safflower oil
finely grated zest and juice of 1 lime
1 red chile, seeded and finely chopped
1 teaspoon sugar
3 tablespoons chopped fresh cilantro
salt

1 Cut the fish into even strips and place them on a plate or in a shallow bowl.

2 To make the marinade, crush the coriander, fennel and cumin seeds with the sugar. Add the chili sauce, garlic oil and salt and combine.

3 Spread the marinade on the fish, cover and let stand in a cool place for at least 20 minutes—longer if you have time.

4 To make the dressing, place the coconut milk and salt in a screw-top jar with 3 tablespoons boiling water and let dissolve. Add the oil, lime zest and juice, chile, sugar and chopped cilantro. Shake well and set aside.

5 Combine the lettuce leaves with the papaya or mango, tomato, cucumber and scallions. Toss with the dressing, then distribute among four large serving plates.

6 Heat a large non-stick frying pan, add the fish and cook for 5 minutes, turning once. Place the cooked fish on the salad and serve immediately.

COOK'S TIP

If planning ahead, you can let the fish in the marinade sit in the refrigerator for up to 8 hours. The dressing can also be made in advance, minus the fresh cilantro. Store at room temperature and add the cilantro when you are ready to assemble the salad.

San Francisco Salad

California is a salad-maker's paradise and is renowned for its great produce. San Francisco has become the salad capital of California, although this recipe is in fact based on a salad served at the Chez Panisse restaurant in Berkeley.

INGREDIENTS

Serves 4

2 pounds langoustines or small
    crayfish

2 ounces fennel, sliced

2 ripe medium-sized tomatoes, quartered,
    and 4 small tomatoes

2 tablespoons olive oil, plus extra for
    moistening the salad leaves

4 tablespoons brandy

⅔ cup dry white wine

1 can (7 ounces) lobster or crab bisque

2 tablespoons chopped fresh tarragon

3 tablespoons heavy cream

8 ounces green beans, trimmed

2 oranges

6 ounces mache

4 ounces arugula leaves

½ frisée lettuce

salt and cayenne pepper

1 Bring a large saucepan of salted water to a boil, add the langoustines or crayfish and simmer for 10 minutes. Refresh under cold running water.

2 Preheat the oven to 425°F. Twist the tails from all but four of the langoustines—reserve these to garnish the dish. Peel the outer shell from the tail meat. Put the tail peelings, carapace and claws in a heavy roasting pan with the fennel and medium-sized tomatoes. Toss with the olive oil and roast near the top of the oven for 20 minutes to bring out the flavors.

3 Remove the roasting pan from the oven and place it over medium heat on top of the stove. Add the brandy and ignite to release the flavor of the alcohol. Add the wine and simmer briefly.

4 Transfer the contents of the roasting pan to a food processor and reduce to a coarse purée: this will take 10–15 seconds. Rub the purée through a fine nylon sieve into a bowl. Add the lobster or crab bisque, tarragon and cream. Season to taste with salt and a little cayenne pepper.

5 Bring a saucepan of salted water to a boil and cook the beans for 6 minutes. Drain and cool under running water. To segment the oranges, cut the peel from the top and bottom, and then from the sides, with a serrated knife. Loosen the segments by cutting between the membranes and the flesh with a small knife.

6 Moisten the salad leaves with olive oil and distribute between four serving plates. Fold the langoustine tails into the dressing and distribute among the plates. Add the beans, orange segments and small tomatoes. Garnish each plate with a whole langoustine and serve warm.

Millionaire's Lobster Salad

When money is no object and you're in a decadent mood, this salad will satisfy your every whim.

INGREDIENTS

Serves 4

1 medium lobster, live or cooked

1 bay leaf

1 fresh thyme sprig

1½ pounds new potatoes, scrubbed

2 ripe tomatoes

4 oranges

½ frisée lettuce

6 ounces mache

4 tablespoons extra-virgin olive oil

1 can (7 ounces) young artichokes
   hearts, quartered

1 small bunch fresh tarragon, chervil or
   flat-leaf parsley

salt

For the dressing

2 tablespoons frozen concentrated orange
   juice, thawed

6 tablespoons unsalted butter, diced

salt and cayenne pepper

1 If the lobster needs cooking, add to a large pan of boiling salted water with the bay leaf and thyme. Bring back to a boil and simmer for 15 minutes. Cool under running water.

2 Twist off the legs and claws, and separate the tail from the body. Break the claws with a hammer and remove the meat. Cut the tail piece open from the underside, slice the meat and set aside.

3 Bring the potatoes to a boil in salted water and simmer for about 15 minutes, until tender. Drain, cover and keep warm.

4 Cut a cross in the skin of the tomatoes, cover with boiling water and set aside for 30 seconds. Cool under running water and slip off the skins. Halve the tomatoes, discard the seeds, then cut the flesh into large dice.

5 To segment the oranges, remove the peel from the top, bottom and sides with a serrated knife. With a small paring knife, loosen the orange segments by cutting between the flesh and the membranes, holding the fruit over a small bowl.

6 To make the dressing, measure the orange juice into a heatproof bowl and set it over a saucepan containing 1 inch simmering water. Heat the juice for 1 minute, turn off the heat, then whisk in the butter a little at a time until the dressing reaches coating consistency.

7 Season to taste with salt and a pinch of cayenne pepper, cover and keep warm.

8 Dress the salad leaves with olive oil, then divide among four large serving plates. Moisten the potatoes, artichokes and orange segments with olive oil and distribute among the leaves.

9 Lay the sliced lobster on the salad, spoon on the warm dressing, add the diced tomato and decorate with the fresh herbs. Serve at room temperature.

Genoese Squid Salad

This is a good salad for summer, when green beans and new potatoes are at their best. Serve it for a first course or light lunch.

INGREDIENTS

Serves 4–6

1 pound prepared squid, cut into rings

4 garlic cloves, roughly chopped

1¼ cups Italian red wine

1 pound waxy new potatoes, scrubbed

8 ounces green beans, trimmed and cut into short lengths

2–3 sun-dried tomatoes in oil, drained and thinly sliced lengthwise

4 tablespoons extra-virgin olive oil

1 tablespoon red wine vinegar

salt and ground black pepper

1 Preheat the oven to 350°F. Put the squid rings in an earthenware dish with half the garlic, the wine and pepper to taste. Cover and cook for 45 minutes or until the squid is tender.

2 Put the potatoes in a saucepan, cover with cold water and add a good pinch of salt. Bring to a boil, cover and simmer for about 15 minutes, until tender. Using a slotted spoon, lift out the potatoes and set aside. Add the beans to the boiling water and cook for 3 minutes. Drain.

3 When the potatoes are cool enough to handle, slice them thickly on the diagonal and place them in a bowl with the warm beans and sun-dried tomatoes. Whisk the oil, vinegar and the remaining garlic in a bowl and add salt and pepper to taste. Pour this over the potato mixture.

4 Drain the squid and discard the liquid. Add the squid to the potato mixture and mix very gently. Arrange on individual plates and season liberally with pepper.

COOK'S TIP

The French potato called Charlotte is perfect for this salad because it retains its shape when boiled. Prepared squid can be bought at supermarkets with fresh fish counters, and at fishmongers.

Tuna Carpaccio

Fillet of beef is most often used for carpaccio, but meaty fish like tuna—and swordfish—make an unusual change. The secret is to slice the fish wafer-thin, made possible by freezing it first, a technique used by the Japanese for making sashimi.

INGREDIENTS

Serves 4

2 fresh tuna steaks, about 1 pound
   total weight
4 tablespoons extra-virgin olive oil
1 tablespoon balsamic vinegar
1 teaspoon sugar
2 tablespoons bottled green peppercorns
   or capers, drained
salt and ground black pepper
lemon wedges and green salad, to serve

1 Remove the skin from each tuna steak and place each steak between two sheets of plastic wrap or non-stick baking paper. Pound with a rolling pin until the steak is flattened slightly.

2 Roll up the tuna steaks as tightly as possible, then wrap tightly in plastic wrap. Place the tuna steaks in the freezer for 4 hours, or until firm.

3 Unwrap the tuna and cut crosswise into the thinnest possible slices. Arrange the slices on individual serving plates.

4 Whisk together the oil, vinegar, sugar and peppercorns or capers, season and pour over the tuna. Cover and let come to room temperature for 30 minutes before serving with lemon wedges and green salad.

COOK'S TIP

Raw fish is safe to eat as long as it is very fresh, so check with your fishmonger before purchasing and make and serve the carpaccio the same day. Do not buy fish that has been frozen and thawed.

Salade Mouclade

Mouclade is a long-established dish from La Rochelle in southwestern France. The dish consists of mussels in a light curry cream sauce, and is usually served hot. Here the flavors appear in a salad of warm lentils and lightly cooked spinach. Serve at room temperature during the summer months.

INGREDIENTS

Serves 4

3 tablespoons olive oil

1 medium onion, finely chopped

1½ cups puy or green lentils, soaked for
    2 hours and drained

3¾ cups vegetable stock

4½ pounds fresh mussels in their shells

5 tablespoons white wine

½ teaspoon curry paste

pinch of saffron

2 tablespoons heavy cream

2 large carrots, peeled

4 celery stalks

2 pounds baby spinach, stems removed

1 tablespoon garlic oil

salt and cayenne pepper

1 Heat the oil in a heavy saucepan and soften the onion for 6–8 minutes. Add the lentils and vegetable stock, bring to a boil and simmer for 45 minutes. Remove from the heat and cool.

2 Clean the mussels thoroughly, discarding any that are damaged. Any that are open should close if given a sharp tap; if they fail to do so, discard these too.

3 Place the mussels in a large saucepan, add the wine, cover and steam over high heat for 12 minutes. Strain the mussels in a colander, collecting the cooking liquor in a bowl, and discard any that have not opened during the cooking. Take all but four of the mussels out of their shells.

4 Pass the mussel liquor through a fine sieve or muslin into a wide, shallow pan to remove any grit or sand.

5 Add the curry paste and saffron, then reduce over high heat until almost dry. Remove from the heat, stir in the cream, season and combine with the mussels.

6 Cut the carrot and celery into 2-inch matchsticks and cook in salted boiling water for 3 minutes. Drain, cool and moisten with olive oil.

7 Wash the spinach, put the wet leaves into a large saucepan, cover and steam for 30 seconds. Immerse in cold water, then press the leaves dry in a colander. Moisten with garlic oil and season.

8 Spoon the lentils into the center of four plates. Place heaps of spinach around the edge, with some carrot and celery on top. Spoon on the mussels and garnish with the reserved mussels in their shells.

Hot Coconut, Shrimp and Papaya Salad

Transport yourself to the Far East with this wonderful dish that combines juicy papaya and succulent shrimp tails in a spicy coconut dressing.

INGREDIENTS

Serves 4–6

8 ounces raw or cooked shrimp tails, peeled and deveined

2 ripe papayas

8 ounces Romaine or iceberg lettuce leaves, Chinese cabbage and baby spinach

1 firm tomato, peeled, seeded and roughly chopped

3 scallions, shredded

1 small bunch fresh cilantro, shredded, and 1 large chile, sliced, to garnish

For the dressing

1 tablespoon coconut milk

6 tablespoons vegetable oil

juice of 1 lime

¹/₂ teaspoon hot chili sauce

2 teaspoons Thai fish sauce (optional)

1 teaspoon sugar

2 If using raw shrimp tails, cover with cold water in a saucepan, bring to a boil and simmer for no longer than 2 minutes. Drain and set aside.

3 Cut the papayas in half from top to bottom and remove the black seeds. Peel off the skin and cut the flesh into equal-sized pieces.

4 Place the salad leaves in a bowl. Add the shrimp, papayas, tomato and scallions. Pour on the dressing, garnish with the cilantro and chile, and serve.

1 To make the dressing, place the coconut milk in a screw-top jar and add 2 tablespoons boiling water to soften it. Add the oil, lime juice, chili sauce, fish sauce, if using, and sugar. Shake well and set aside. Do not chill.

Roasted Chicken and Walnut Salad

The chickens may be cooked the day before eating and the salad finished on the day itself. Serve with warm garlic bread.

INGREDIENTS

Serves 8

4 fresh tarragon or rosemary sprigs
2 x 4–4½-pound chickens
5 tablespoons butter
⅔ cup chicken stock
⅔ cup white wine
1 cup walnut pieces
1 small cantaloupe
lettuce leaves
1 pound seedless grapes or pitted cherries
salt and ground black pepper

For the dressing

2 tablespoons tarragon vinegar
½ cup light olive oil
2 tablespoons chopped fresh mixed herbs
    such as parsley, mint, tarragon

1 Preheat the oven to 400°F. Put the sprigs of tarragon or rosemary inside the chickens and season with salt and pepper.

2 Spread the chickens with 4 tablespoons of the softened butter, place in a roasting pan and pour the stock around. Cover loosely with foil and roast for 1½ hours, basting twice, until browned and the juices run clear. Remove from the roasting pan and let cool.

3 Add the wine to the roasting pan. Bring to a boil on the stove and cook until syrupy. Strain and let cool. Heat the remaining butter in a frying pan and gently fry the walnuts until lightly browned. Scoop the melon flesh into balls or cut into cubes. Joint the chickens.

4 To make the dressing, whisk the vinegar and olive oil together with a little salt and pepper. Remove the fat from the chicken juices and add the juices to the dressing with the herbs. Adjust the seasoning to taste.

5 Arrange the chicken pieces on a bed of lettuce leaves, sprinkle on the grapes or cherries and melon, and spoon on the dressing. Sprinkle with the toasted walnuts and serve.

Chicken Liver Salad

This delicious salad may be served as a main course for a summer lunch party, or as a tasty first course served on individual plates. The richness of the chicken livers is complemented perfectly by the sweet and tangy whole-grain mustard dressing. Serve with warm crusty bread to mop up the dressing.

INGREDIENTS

Serves 4

mixed salad leaves such as frisée, oak leaf lettuce, radicchio
1 avocado, diced
2 tablespoons lemon juice
2 pink grapefruit
12 ounces chicken livers
2 tablespoons olive oil
1 garlic clove, crushed
salt and ground black pepper
whole fresh chives, to garnish

For the dressing
2 tablespoons lemon juice
4 tablespoons olive oil
1/2 teaspoon whole-grain mustard
1/2 teaspoon honey
1 tablespoon snipped fresh chives
salt and ground black pepper

1 To make the dressing, put the lemon juice, olive oil, mustard, honey and fresh chives into a screw-top jar, and shake vigorously. Season to taste with salt and freshly ground black pepper.

2 Arrange the previously washed and well-drained mixed salad leaves attractively on a large serving plate.

3 Peel and dice the avocado and mix with the lemon juice to prevent browning. Add to the plate of mixed leaves.

4 Peel the grapefruit, removing as much of the white pith as possible. Split into segments and arrange with the leaves and avocado on the serving plate.

5 Dry the chicken livers on paper towels and remove any unwanted pieces.

6 Using a sharp knife, cut the larger chicken livers in half. Leave the smaller ones whole.

7 Heat the oil in a large frying pan. Stir-fry the chicken livers and garlic briskly until the livers are brown all over (they should be slightly pink inside).

8 Season the chicken livers to taste with salt and black pepper, remove from the pan and drain on paper towels.

9 Place the chicken livers, while still warm, onto the salad leaves and spoon on the dressing. Garnish with the whole chives and serve immediately.

Grilled Chicken Salad with Lavender

Lavender may seem an odd salad ingredient, but its delightful scent has a natural affinity with garlic, orange and other herbs. A serving of polenta makes this salad both filling and delicious.

INGREDIENTS

Serves 4

4 boneless chicken breasts

3¾ cups light chicken stock

1 cup fine polenta or cornmeal

4 tablespoons butter

1 pound baby spinach

6 ounces mache

8 small tomatoes, halved

salt and ground black pepper

8 fresh lavender sprigs, to garnish

For the lavender marinade

6 fresh lavender flowers

2 teaspoons finely grated orange zest

2 garlic cloves, crushed

2 teaspoons honey

2 tablespoons olive oil

2 teaspoons chopped fresh thyme

2 teaspoons chopped fresh marjoram

salt

1 To make the marinade, strip the lavender flowers from their stems and combine with the orange zest, garlic, honey and a pinch of salt. Add the olive oil, thyme and marjoram. Slash the chicken deeply, spread on the mixture and let marinate in a cool place for at least 20 minutes.

2 To make the polenta, bring the chicken stock to a boil in a heavy saucepan. Add the fine polenta or cornmeal in a steady stream, stirring constantly until thick: This will take 2–3 minutes. Transfer the cooked polenta to a 1 inch deep buttered tray and let cool.

3 Heat the broiler to medium. (If using a barbecue, let the embers settle to a steady glow.) Grill the chicken breasts for about 15 minutes, turning them once.

4 Cut the cooled polenta into 1-inch cubes with a wet knife. Heat the remaining butter in a large frying-pan and fry the polenta cubes until golden brown.

5 Divide the salad leaves and tomatoes between four large serving plates. Slice each chicken breast and lay over the salad. Place the polenta cubes among the salad and season to taste. Garnish with the sprigs of lavender and serve.

COOK'S TIP

This lavender marinade is a delicious flavoring for salt-water fish as well as chicken. Try it spread on grilled cod, haddock, halibut or sea bass.

Dijon Chicken Salad

This attractive and classical dish is ideal to serve for a simple but tasty and elegant lunch. Serve with extra salad leaves and some warm herb and garlic bread.

Serves 4

4 skinless, boneless chicken breasts
mixed salad leaves such as frisée, oak leaf
    lettuce, radicchio

For the marinade
2 tablespoons tarragon wine vinegar
1 teaspoon Dijon mustard
1 teaspoon honey
6 tablespoons olive oil
salt and ground black pepper

For the mustard dressing
2 tablespoons Dijon mustard
3 garlic cloves, crushed
1 tablespoon grated onion
4 tablespoons white wine

1 To make the marinade, combine the vinegar, mustard, honey, olive oil, salt and pepper in a shallow glass or earthenware dish that is large enough to hold the chicken breasts in a single layer.

2 Add the chicken breasts to the dish, making sure they do not overlap each other.

3 Turn the chicken over in the marinade to coat completely, cover with plastic wrap and chill in the refrigerator overnight.

4 Preheat the oven to 375°F. Transfer the chicken and the marinade to an ovenproof dish, cover with tinfoil and bake for about 35 minutes or until tender. Let the chicken cool in the liquid.

5 To make the mustard dressing, put all the ingredients into a screw-top jar and shake vigorously.

6 Thinly slice the chicken, and fan out the slices.

7 Arrange the chicken slices on a serving dish with the salad leaves. Spoon on some of the mustard dressing and serve. Serve the rest of the dressing separately in a bowl or pitcher.

COOK'S TIP

The dressing can be made several days in advance and stored in the refrigerator.

Duck Breast and Pasta Salad

The acidity of fruit is a very good accompaniment to a rich meat like duck, as it adds a tartness that makes the meat more digestible. This luxurious salad includes apple, orange and, in the dressing, dried cherries. The pasta adds a welcome element of carbohydrate and makes the dish a complete meal.

INGREDIENTS

Serves 6

2 boneless duck breasts

1 teaspoon coriander seeds, crushed

12 ounces rigatoni

1 apple, diced

2 oranges, segmented

salt and ground black pepper

extra fresh chopped cilantro and mint,
    to garnish

For the dressing

⅔ cup orange juice

1 tablespoon lemon juice

2 teaspoons honey

1 shallot, finely chopped

1 garlic clove, crushed

1 celery stalk, chopped

3 ounces dried cherries

3 tablespoons port

1 tablespoon chopped fresh mint

2 tablespoons chopped fresh cilantro

1 Preheat the oven to 375°F. Remove the skin and fat from the duck breasts, season with salt and pepper and rub with the crushed coriander seeds.

2 Bake the duck breasts for 7–10 minutes (depending on the size). Wrap the duck breasts in foil and set aside for 20 minutes.

3 Cook the pasta in a large pan of salted, boiling water, until *al dente*. Drain thoroughly and rinse under cold running water. Let the pasta cool.

4 To make the dressing, put the orange juice, lemon juice, honey, shallot, garlic, celery, cherries, port, mint and fresh cilantro into a small bowl. Whisk together and let marinate for 30 minutes.

5 Unwrap the breasts from the foil and, using a very sharp carving knife, slice the duck very thinly. (It should still be slightly pink in the center.)

6 Put the pasta into a mixing bowl, and add the dressing, diced apple and segments of orange. Toss well to coat the pasta.

7 Transfer the salad to a serving plate with the duck slices and garnish with the extra cilantro and mint.

Duck Salad with Orange Sauce

The rich, gamy flavor of duck provides the foundation for this delicious salad. Serve it in late summer or autumn and enjoy the warm flavors of orange and cilantro. Garlic croûtons add extra crunchy texture.

INGREDIENTS

Serves 4

1 small orange

2 boneless duck breasts

⅔ cup dry white wine

1 teaspoon ground coriander seeds

½ teaspoon ground cumin or fennel seeds

2 tablespoons sugar

juice of ½ small lime or lemon

3 ounces day-old bread, thickly sliced

3 tablespoons garlic oil

½ escarole lettuce

½ frisée lettuce

2 tablespoons sunflower or peanut oil

salt and cayenne pepper

4 sprigs fresh cilantro, to garnish

1 Halve the orange and slice thickly. Discard any seeds and place the slices in a small saucepan. Cover with water, bring to a boil and simmer for 5 minutes to remove the bitterness. Drain the orange slices and set aside.

2 Pierce the skin of the duck breasts diagonally with a small knife (this will help release the fat). Rub the skin with salt.

3 Place a steel or cast-iron frying pan over steady heat and cook the breasts for 20 minutes, turning once, until they are medium-rare. Transfer to a warm plate, cover and keep warm.

4 Heat the sediment in the frying pan until it begins to darken and caramelize. Add the wine and stir to loosen the sediment. Add the ground coriander, cumin or fennel seeds, sugar and orange slices.

5 Boil quickly and reduce to coating consistency. Sharpen with the lime or lemon juice and season to taste with salt and cayenne pepper. Transfer the orange sauce to a bowl, cover and keep warm.

6 Remove the crusts from the bread and cut the bread into short fingers. Heat the garlic oil in a heavy frying pan and brown the croûtons. Season with salt, then transfer to paper towels.

7 Moisten the salad leaves with a little sunflower or peanut oil and distribute among four large serving plates.

8 Slice the duck breasts diagonally with a carving knife. Divide the meat into fourths and lift onto each salad plate. Spoon on the orange sauce, sprinkle with croûtons, decorate with a sprig of fresh cilantro and serve warm.

Sesame Duck and Noodle Salad

This salad is complete in itself and makes a lovely summer lunch. The marinade is a delicious blend of Asian flavors.

INGREDIENTS

Serves 4

2 boneless duck breasts

1 tablespoon oil

5 ounces sugar snap peas

2 carrots, cut into 3-inch sticks

8 ounces medium egg noodles

6 scallions, sliced

salt

2 tablespoons fresh cilantro leaves, to garnish

For the marinade

1 tablespoon sesame oil

1 teaspoon ground coriander

1 teaspoon five-spice powder

For the dressing

1 tablespoon vinegar

1 teaspoon light brown sugar

1 teaspoon soy sauce

1 garlic clove, crushed

1 tablespoon sesame seeds, toasted

3 tablespoons sunflower oil

2 tablespoons sesame oil

ground black pepper

1 Slice the duck breasts thinly across and place in a shallow dish. Combine the ingredients for the marinade, pour onto the duck and turn well to coat thoroughly. Cover and let sit in a cool place for 30 minutes.

2 Heat the oil in a frying pan, add the slices of duck breast and stir-fry for 3–4 minutes, until cooked. Set aside.

3 Bring a saucepan of lightly salted water to a boil. Place the sugar snap peas and carrots in a steamer that will fit on top of the pan. When the water boils, add the noodles. Place the steamer on top and steam the vegetables while cooking the noodles.

4 Set the steamed vegetables aside. Drain the noodles, refresh under cold running water and drain again. Place them in a large serving bowl.

5 To make the dressing, mix the vinegar, sugar, soy sauce, garlic and sesame seeds in a bowl. Add a generous grinding of pepper, then whisk in the oils.

6 Pour the dressing on the noodles and mix well. Add the peas, carrots, scallions and duck slices and toss to mix. Sprinkle the cilantro leaves on top and serve immediately.

Prosciutto Salad with an Avocado Fan

Avocados are amazingly versatile—they can serve as edible containers, be sliced or diced in a salad, or form the foundation of a delicious soup or sauce. However, they are at their most elegant when sliced thinly and fanned on a plate.

INGREDIENTS

Serves 4

3 avocados

5 ounces prosciutto

3–4 ounces arugula leaves

24 marinated black olives, drained

For the dressing

1 tablespoon balsamic vinegar

1 teaspoon lemon juice

1 teaspoon mustard

1 teaspoon sugar

5 tablespoons olive oil

salt and ground black pepper

1 To make the dressing, combine the balsamic vinegar, lemon juice, mustard and sugar in a bowl. Whisk in the oil, season to taste and set aside.

2 Cut two of the avocados in half. Remove the pits and skins, and cut the flesh into ½-inch slices. Toss with half the dressing. Place the prosciutto, avocado slices and arugula on four serving plates. Sprinkle the olives and the remaining dressing on top.

3 Halve, pit and peel the remaining avocado. Slice each half lengthwise into eighths. Gently draw a sharp knife across the quarters at ½-inch intervals to create regular stripes.

4 Make four cuts lengthwise down each avocado eighth, leaving ½ inch intact at the end. Carefully fan out the slices and arrange on the side of each plate.

Melon and Prosciutto Salad

Sections of cool, fragrant melon covered with slices of prosciutto make this a delicious appetizer. When fresh strawberries are in season, serve it with a savory-sweet strawberry salsa.

Serves 4

1 large melon (cantaloupe, Galia or
    Charentais)
6 ounces prosciutto, thinly sliced

For the salsa

8 ounces strawberries
1 teaspoon sugar
2 tablespoons peanut or sunflower oil
1 tablespoon orange juice
½ teaspoon finely grated orange zest
½ teaspoon grated fresh ginger
salt and ground black pepper

1 Halve the melon and take the seeds out with a spoon. Cut the zest off with a paring knife, then slice the melon flesh thickly. Chill until ready to serve.

2 To make the salsa, hull the strawberries and cut them into large dice. Place in a small mixing bowl with the sugar, and crush lightly to release the juices. Add the oil, orange juice and zest and ginger. Season with salt and a generous twist of black pepper.

3 Arrange the melon slices on a serving plate and lay the prosciutto over the top. Serve the salsa separately in a small bowl.

Wild Mushroom Salad with Prosciutto

Autumn provides a wealth of ingredients for the salad maker. Most treasured of all are wild mushrooms, found mainly in deciduous woodland. If you are not familiar with edible species, larger supermarkets and specialty stores often sell a wide range.

INGREDIENTS

Serves 4

6 ounces prosciutto, thickly sliced

3 tablespoons butter

1 pound wild or cultivated mushrooms such as chanterelles and oyster mushrooms, sliced

4 tablespoons brandy

½ oak leaf lettuce

½ frisée lettuce

1 tablespoon walnut oil

salt and ground black pepper

For the herb pancake

3 tablespoons flour

5 tablespoons milk

1 egg, plus 1 egg yolk

4 tablespoons grated Parmesan cheese

3 tablespoons chopped fresh mixed herbs such as parsley, thyme, tarragon, marjoram, chives

salt and ground black pepper

1 To make the pancakes, combine the flour with the milk in a bowl. Beat in the egg and egg yolk with the Parmesan cheese, herbs and seasoning. Place a non-stick frying pan over a steady heat. Pour in enough mixture to coat the bottom of the pan.

2 When the batter has set, turn the pancake over and cook briefly on the other side. Remove the pancake and let cool. Continue until you have used all the batter.

3 Roll the pancakes together and cut into ½-inch ribbons. Cut the prosciutto into similar-sized ribbons and toss with the pancake ribbons.

4 Heat the butter in a frying pan until it begins to foam. Add the mushrooms and cook for 6–8 minutes. Add the brandy and ignite with a match. The flames will subside when the alcohol has burnt off. Moisten the salad leaves with walnut oil and distribute between four serving plates. Place the ham and pancake ribbons in the center, spoon on the mushrooms, season and serve warm.

Beef and Herbed Pasta Salad

Lean, tender beef is marinated with ginger and garlic, then lightly grilled and served warm with an herbed pasta salad.

INGREDIENTS

Serves 6

1 pound beef fillet

1 pound fresh tagliatelle with sun-dried tomatoes and herbs

4 ounces cherry tomatoes

½ cucumber

For the marinade

1 tablespoon soy sauce

1 tablespoon sherry

1 teaspoon grated fresh ginger

1 garlic clove, crushed

For the herb dressing

2–3 tablespoons horseradish sauce

⅔ cup plain yogurt

1 garlic clove, crushed

2–3 tablespoons chopped fresh mixed herbs such as chives, parsley, thyme

salt and ground black pepper

1 To make the marinade, combine all the ingredients in a shallow dish. Add the beef fillet and turn to coat well. Cover with plastic wrap and let sit for 30 minutes to let the flavors penetrate the meat.

2 Preheat the grill. Lift the fillet out of the marinade and pat it dry with paper towels. Place the fillet on a grill rack and grill for 8 minutes on each side, basting with the marinade during cooking.

3 Transfer the fillet to a plate, cover with foil and let stand for 20 minutes.

4 To make the herb dressing, put all the ingredients into a bowl and mix thoroughly. Cook the pasta until it is *al dente*, drain thoroughly, rinse under cold water and let dry.

5 Cut the cherry tomatoes in half. Cut the cucumber in half lengthwise, scoop out the seeds with a teaspoon and slice the flesh thinly into crescents.

6 Put the pasta, tomatoes, cucumber and dressing into a mixing bowl and toss to coat. Slice the beef and arrange on individual serving plates with the pasta salad. Serve warm.

Burger Salad with Sesame Croûtons

This salad plays on the ingredients that make up the all-American burger in a sesame seed bun. Inside the burger is a layer of Roquefort, the blue sheep's-milk cheese from France.

INGREDIENTS

Serves 4

2 pounds lean ground beef

1 egg

1 medium onion, finely chopped

2 teaspoons Dijon mustard

½ teaspoon celery salt

4 ounces Roquefort or other blue cheese

1 large loaf sesame seed bread

3 tablespoons olive oil

1 small iceberg lettuce

2 ounces arugula or watercress leaves

½ cup French Dressing

4 ripe tomatoes, quartered

4 large scallions, sliced

ground black pepper

1 Place the ground beef, egg, onion, mustard, celery salt and pepper in a mixing bowl. Combine thoroughly. Divide the mixture into 16 portions, each weighing 2 ounces.

2 Flatten the pieces between two sheets of waxed paper to form 5-inch rounds.

3 Place ½ ounce of the blue cheese on eight of the burgers. Sandwich with the remaining burgers and press the edges firmly. Store between sheets of waxed paper and chill until ready to cook.

4 To make the sesame croûtons, preheat the grill to a medium. Remove the sesame seed crust from the loaf, then cut the crust into short fingers. Moisten with olive oil and toast evenly for 10–15 minutes.

5 Grill the burgers at the same temperature for 10 minutes, turning once.

6 Toss the salad leaves with the French Dressing, then distribute among four large serving plates. Place two burgers in the center of each plate and arrange the tomatoes, scallions and sesame croûtons around the edge.

COOK'S TIP

If you can't find a sesame seed loaf use French bread. Cut the bread into slices about ½ inch thick, brush with olive oil and place on a baking sheet. Bake in the oven at low heat for around 15 minutes, until the bread rounds are crisp and golden.

FRUIT SALADS

~

Fresh Fruit Salad

This basic fruit salad is always welcome, especially after a rich main course. It is endlessly adaptable—when peaches and strawberries are out of season, use bananas and grapes, or any other fruit.

INGREDIENTS

Serves 6

2 apples

2 oranges

2 peaches

16–20 strawberries

2 tablespoons lemon juice

1–2 tablespoons orange flower water

confectioners' sugar (optional)

a few fresh mint leaves, to decorate

1 Peel and core the apples and cut into thin slices. Peel the oranges with a sharp knife, removing all the pith, and segment them, catching the juice in a bowl.

2 Plunge the peaches for 1 minute in boiling water, peel off the skin and cut the flesh into thick slices, discarding the pits.

3 Hull the strawberries and halve or quarter if larger. Place all the fruit in a large serving bowl.

4 Blend the lemon juice, orange flower water and orange juice. Taste and add a little confectioners' sugar to sweeten, if desired. Pour the fruit juice mixture on the salad and serve decorated with mint leaves.

Dried Fruit Salad

This wonderful combination of fresh and dried fruit makes an excellent dessert throughout the year. Use frozen raspberries and blackberries during the winter months.

INGREDIENTS

Serves 4

½ cup dried apricots

½ cup dried peaches

1 pear

1 apple

1 orange

⅔ cup mixed raspberries
   and blackberries

1 cinnamon stick

¼ cup sugar

1 tablespoon honey

1 tablespoon lemon juice

1 Soak the dried apricots and peaches in water for 1–2 hours, until plump, then drain and halve or quarter. Peel and core the pear and apple and cut into cubes.

2 Peel the orange with a sharp knife, removing all the pith, and cut into wedges. Place all the fruit in a large saucepan with the raspberries and blackberries.

3 Add 2½ cups water, the cinnamon stick, sugar and honey and bring to a boil. Cover and simmer very gently for 10–12 minutes, then remove the pan from the heat.

4 Stir in the lemon juice. Let cool, then transfer to a bowl and chill in the refrigerator for 1–2 hours before serving.

Cool Green Fruit Salad

A sophisticated, simple fruit salad for any time of the year.

Serves 6

3 Ogen or Galia melons
4 ounces seedless green grapes
2 kiwi fruits
1 star
1 green apple
1 lime
¾ cup sparkling grape juice

1 Cut the melons in half and remove the seeds. Keeping the shells intact, scoop out the flesh with a melon baller, or scoop it out with a spoon and cut into bite-sized cubes. Reserve the melon shells.

2 Remove any stems from the grapes and, if they are large, cut them in half. Peel and chop the kiwi. Thinly slice the star fruit. Core and thinly slice the apple and place in a mixing bowl with the melon, grapes, kiwi fruit and star fruit.

3 Thinly pare the zest from the lime and cut it in fine strips. Blanch the lime strips in boiling water for 30 seconds, drain and rinse in cold water. Squeeze the juice from the lime and toss the juice into the bowl of fruit.

4 Spoon the prepared fruit into the reserved melon shells, and chill the shells in the refrigerator until needed. Just before serving, spoon the sparkling grape juice onto the fruit and sprinkle with the strips of lime zest.

COOK'S TIP

On a hot summer's day, serve the filled melon shells on a platter of crushed ice to keep them beautifully cool.

Winter Fruit Salad

This is a colorful, refreshing and nutritious fruit salad, which is ideal served with plain yogurt or cream.

INGREDIENTS

Serves 6

1 can (8 ounces) pineapple chunks in
    fruit juice

scant 1 cup freshly squeezed orange juice

scant 1 cup unsweetened apple juice

2 tablespoons orange or apple liqueur

2 tablespoons honey (optional)

2 oranges, peeled

2 green apples, chopped

2 pears, chopped

4 plums, pitted and chopped

12 fresh dates, pitted and chopped

½ cup dried apricots

fresh mint sprigs, to decorate

1 Drain the pineapple, reserving the juice. Put the pineapple juice, orange juice, apple juice, liqueur and honey, if using, in a large serving bowl and stir.

COOK'S TIP

Use other unsweetened fruit juices such as pink grapefruit and pineapple juice in place of the orange and apple juice.

2 Segment the oranges, catching any juice in the bowl. Put the orange segments and pineapple in the fruit juice mixture.

3 Add the chopped apples and pears to the bowl.

4 Stir in the plums, dates and dried apricots, cover and chill for several hours. Decorate with fresh mint sprigs to serve.

Italian Fruit Salad and Ice Cream

If you visit Italy in the summer, you will find little fruit shops selling small dishes of macerated berries, which are delectable on their own, but also are great with ice cream.

INGREDIENTS

Serves 6

2 pounds mixed summer fruit such as strawberries, raspberries, red currants, blueberries, peaches, apricots, plums, melons

juice of 3–4 oranges

juice of 1 lemon

1 tablespoon concentrated pear or apple juice

4 tablespoons whipping cream

2 tablespoons orange liqueur (optional)

fresh mint sprigs, to decorate

1 Prepare the fruit according to type. Cut it into reasonably small pieces.

2 Put the fruit into a serving bowl and pour on enough orange juice to cover. Add the lemon juice and chill for 2 hours.

3 Set half the macerated fruit aside to serve as it is. Purée the remainder in a blender or food processor.

4 Gently warm the pear or apple juice and stir into the fruit purée. Whip the cream and fold it in, then add the liqueur, if using.

5 Churn the mixture in an ice-cream maker. Alternatively, place it in a suitable container for freezing. Freeze until ice crystals form around the edge, then beat the mixture until smooth.

6 Repeat the process once or twice, then freeze until firm.

7 Soften slightly in the refrigerator before serving with the fruit decorated with sprigs of mint.

COOK'S TIP

The macerated fruit also makes a delicious drink. Purée in a blender or food processor, then press through a sieve.

Watermelon, Ginger and Grapefruit Salad

This pretty, pink combination is very light and refreshing for any summer meal.

Serves 4

2 cups watermelon flesh

2 ruby or pink grapefruit

2 pieces stem ginger and
   2 tablespoons of the syrup

1 Remove any seeds from the watermelon and cut the flesh into bite-sized chunks.

2 Using a small, sharp knife, cut off all the peel and white pith from the grapefruit and carefully lift out the segments, catching any juice in a bowl.

COOK'S TIP

Toss the fruits gently—grapefruit segments will break up easily and the appearance of the dish will be spoiled.

3 Finely chop the stem ginger and place in a serving bowl with the melon cubes and grapefruit segments, adding the reserved juice.

4 Spoon on the ginger syrup and toss the fruits lightly to mix. Chill before serving.

Fresh Fruit with Mango Coulis

Fruit sauce, or coulis, became very fashionable in the 1970s with nouvelle cuisine. This bright, flavorful sauce is easy to prepare and ideal for making a simple fruit salad seem special.

INGREDIENTS

Serves 6

1 large ripe mango, peeled, pitted
    and chopped

zest of 1 orange

juice of 3 oranges

sugar, to taste

2 peaches

2 nectarines

1 small mango, peeled

2 plums

1 pear or ½ small melon

juice of 1 lemon

1–2 ounces heaping tablespoons wild
    strawberries (optional)

1–2 ounces heaping tablespoons raspberries

1–2 ounces heaping tablespoons
    blueberries

small fresh mint sprigs, to decorate

1 In a food processor fitted with a metal blade, blend the large mango until smooth. Add the orange zest and juice and sugar to taste and process again until very smooth. Press through a sieve into a bowl and chill.

2 Slice and pit the peaches, nectarines, small mango and plums. Quarter the pear and remove the core or, if using, slice the melon thinly and remove the skin.

3 Place the sliced fruits on a large plate, sprinkle with the lemon juice and chill, covered with plastic wrap, for up to 3 hours before serving. (Some fruits discolor if cut too far ahead of time.)

4 To serve, arrange the sliced fruits on serving plates, spoon the berries on top, drizzle with a little mango coulis and decorate with mint sprigs. Serve the remaining coulis separately.

Fruits-of-the-Tropics Salad

This is a creamy, exotic fruit salad flavored with coconut and spices.

INGREDIENTS

Serves 4–6

1 medium pineapple

1 can (14 ounces) guava halves in syrup

2 medium bananas, sliced

1 large mango, peeled, pitted and diced

4 ounces stem ginger and
   2 tablespoons of the syrup

4 tablespoons coconut milk

2 teaspoon sugar

½ teaspoon grated nutmeg

½ teaspoon ground cinnamon

strips of coconut, to decorate

1 Peel, core and cube the pineapple, and place in a serving bowl. Drain the guavas, reserving the syrup, and chop. Add the guavas to the bowl with one of the bananas and the mango.

2 Chop the stem ginger and add to the pineapple mixture.

3 Pour the 2 tablespoons of the ginger syrup and the reserved guava syrup into a blender or food processor and add the remaining banana, the coconut milk and the sugar. Blend to make a smooth, creamy purée.

4 Pour the banana and coconut purée onto the fruit and add a little grated nutmeg and a sprinkling of cinnamon on top. Serve chilled, decorated with strips of coconut.

Exotic Fruit Salad

A variety of fruits can be used for this salad depending on what is available. Look for fresh mandarin oranges, star fruit, papaya, Cape gooseberries and passion fruit.

INGREDIENTS

Serves 4

scant ½ cup sugar

2 tablespoons stem ginger syrup

2 pieces star anise

1-inch piece cinnamon stick

1 clove

juice of ½ lemon

2 fresh mint sprigs

1 mango

2 bananas

8 lychees, fresh or canned

2 cups strawberries

2 pieces stem ginger, cut into sticks

1 medium pineapple

1 Place the sugar in a saucepan and add 1¼ cups water, the ginger syrup, spices, lemon juice and mint. Bring to a boil and simmer for 3 minutes. Strain into a large bowl.

2 Remove both the top and bottom from the mango and remove the outer skin. Stand the mango on one end and remove the flesh in two pieces on either side of the flat pit. Slice evenly and add to the syrup. Add the bananas, lychees, strawberries and ginger. Chill until ready to serve.

3 Cut the pineapple in half down the center. Loosen the flesh with a small, serrated knife and remove to form two boat shapes. Cut the pineapple flesh into large chunks and place in the cooled syrup.

4 Spoon the fruit salad carefully into the pineapple halves and bring to the table on a large serving dish or board. There will be enough fruit salad left over to refill the pineapple halves for a second serving.

Melon and Strawberry Salad

A beautiful and colorful fruit salad, this is equally suitable to serve as a refreshing appetizer or to round off a meal.

INGREDIENTS

Serves 4

1 Galia melon

1 honeydew melon

½ watermelon

2 cups strawberries

1 tablespoon lemon juice

1 tablespoon honey

1 tablespoon chopped fresh mint

1 fresh mint sprig (optional)

1 Prepare the melons by cutting them in half and discarding the seeds. Use a melon baller to scoop out the flesh into balls or alternatively a knife to cut it into cubes. Place these in a fruit bowl.

2 Rinse and hull the strawberries, cut in half and add to the melon balls or cubes.

COOK'S TIP

Use whichever melons are available: Replace Galia with cantaloupe or watermelon with Charentais, for example. Try to choose three melons with a variation in color for an attractive effect.

3 Combine the lemon juice and honey and add 1 tablespoon water to make it easier to spoon onto the fruit. Mix into the fruit gently.

4 Sprinkle the chopped mint on top of the fruit. Serve the fruit salad decorated with the mint sprig, if desired.

Blueberry, Orange and Lavender Salad

Delicate blueberries feature here in a simple salad of sharp oranges and sweet little meringues flavored with fresh lavender.

INGREDIENTS

Serves 4

6 oranges

3 cups blueberries

8 fresh lavender sprigs, to decorate

For the meringue

2 egg whites

generous ½ cup sugar

1 teaspoon fresh lavender flowers

1 Preheat the oven to 275°F. Line a baking sheet with six layers of newspaper and cover with non-stick baking parchment. To make the meringue, whisk the egg whites in a large mixing bowl until they hold their weight on the whisk. Add the sugar a little at a time, whisking thoroughly before each addition. Fold in the lavender flowers.

2 Spoon the lavender meringue into a piping bag fitted with a ¼-inch plain nozzle. Pipe as many small buttons of meringue onto the prepared baking sheet as you can. Dry the meringues near the bottom of the oven for 1½–2 hours.

3 To segment the oranges, remove the peel from the top, bottom and sides with a serrated knife. Loosen the segments by cutting with a paring knife between the flesh and the membranes, holding the fruit over a bowl.

4 Arrange the orange segments on four plates.

5 Combine the blueberries with the lavender meringues and pile in the center of each plate. Decorate with sprigs of lavender and serve.

Fresh Fig, Apple and Date Salad

Sweet Mediterranean figs and dates combine especially well with crisp apples. A hint of almond serves to unite the flavors.

INGREDIENTS

Serves 4

6 large apples

juice of ½ lemon

generous 1 cup fresh dates

1 ounce marzipan

1 teaspoon orange flower water

4 tablespoons plain yogurt

4 ripe green or purple figs

4 almonds, toasted

1 Core the apples. Slice thinly, then cut into fine matchsticks. Moisten with lemon juice to keep them white.

2 Remove the pits from the dates and cut the flesh into fine strips, then combine them with the apple slices.

3 Soften the marzipan with the orange flower water and combine with the yogurt. Mix well.

4 Pile the apples and dates in the center of four serving plates. Remove the stem from each of the figs and divide the fruit into quarters without cutting right through the base. Squeeze the base with the thumb and forefinger of each hand to open up the fig.

5 Place a fig in the center of each fruit salad, spoon in the yogurt filling and decorate with a toasted almond.

Blackberry Salad with Rose Granita

The blackberry is a member of the rose family and combines especially well with rose water. Here, a rose syrup is frozen into a granita and served over strips of white meringue.

INGREDIENTS

Serves 4

⅔ cup sugar

1 fresh red rose, petals finely chopped

1 teaspoon rose water

2 teaspoons lemon juice

2⅔ cups blackberries

confectioners' sugar, for dusting

fresh rose petals, to decorate

For the meringue

2 egg whites

generous ½ cup sugar

1 To make the granita, bring ⅔ cup water to a boil in a stainless-steel or enamel saucepan. Add the sugar and rose petals, then simmer for 5 minutes.

2 Strain the syrup into a deep metal tray, add another scant 2 cups water, the rose water and lemon juice and let cool. Freeze the mixture for 3 hours or until solid.

3 Meanwhile preheat the oven to 275°F. Line a baking sheet with six layers of newspaper and cover with non-stick baking parchment.

4 To make the meringue, whisk the egg whites until they hold their weight on the whisk. Add the sugar a little at a time, and whisk until firm.

COOK'S TIP

Blackberries are widely cultivated from late spring to autumn and are usually large, plump and sweet. The finest wild blackberries have a bitter edge and a strong depth of flavor —best appreciated with a sprinkling of sugar.

5 Spoon the meringue into a piping bag fitted with a ½-inch plain nozzle. Pipe the meringue in lengths across the paper-lined baking sheet. Dry the meringue near the bottom of the oven for 1½–2 hours.

6 Break the meringue into 2-inch lengths and place three or four pieces on each of four large serving plates. Pile the blackberries next to the meringue.

7 With a tablespoon, scrape the granita finely. Shape into ovals and place on the meringue. Dust with confectioners' sugar, decorate with rose petals, and serve.

Raspberries with Mango Custard

This remarkable salad unites the sharp quality of fresh raspberries with a special custard made from rich, fragrant mangoes.

INGREDIENTS

Serves 4

1 large mango

3 egg yolks

2 tablespoons sugar

2 teaspoons cornstarch

scant 1 cup milk

8 fresh mint sprigs, to decorate

For the raspberry sauce

2⅔ cups raspberries

3 tablespoons sugar

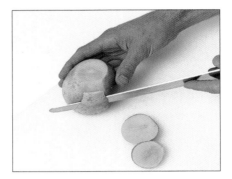

1 To prepare the mango, remove the top and bottom with a serrated knife. Cut off the outer skin, then remove the flesh by cutting on either side of the flat central pit. Save half of the mango flesh for decoration and roughly chop the remainder.

COOK'S TIP

Mangoes are ripe when they yield to gentle pressure. Some varieties show a red-gold or yellow flush when they are ready to eat.

2 For the custard, combine the egg yolks, sugar, cornstarch and 2 tablespoons of the milk smoothly in a small bowl.

3 Rinse a small saucepan with cold water to prevent the milk from catching. Bring the rest of the milk to a boil in the pan, pour it over the ingredients in the bowl and stir evenly.

4 Strain the mixture through a sieve back into the saucepan, stir to the simmering point and let the mixture thicken.

5 Pour the custard into a food processor, add the chopped mango and blend until smooth. Let the custard cool.

6 To make the raspberry sauce, place 2 cups of the raspberries in a stain-resistant saucepan. Add the sugar, soften over low heat and simmer for 5 minutes. Rub the fruit through a fine nylon sieve to remove the seeds. Let cool.

7 Spoon the raspberry sauce and mango custard into two pools on four serving plates. Slice the reserved mango and fan out or arrange in a pattern over the raspberry sauce. Sprinkle the remaining raspberries on the mango custard. Decorate each plate with two sprigs of mint and serve.

Pineapple Crush with Strawberries and Lychees

The sweet, tropical flavors of pineapple and lychees combine well with richly scented strawberries to make this a most refreshing salad.

INGREDIENTS

Serves 4

2 small pineapples

4 cups strawberries

1 can (14 ounces) lychees

3 tablespoons kirsch or white rum

2 tablespoons confectioners' sugar

1 Remove the crowns from both pineapples by twisting sharply. Reserve the leaves for decoration.

2 Cut both pineapples in half diagonally using a large, serrated knife.

3 Cut around the flesh inside the skin of both pineapples with a small, serrated knife, keeping the skin intact. Remove the core from the pineapple and discard. Chop the flesh. Reserve the skins.

4 Hull the strawberries and gently combine with the pineapple and lychees, taking care not to damage the fruit.

5 Mix the kirsch or rum with the confectioners' sugar, pour onto the fruit and freeze for 45 minutes.

6 Transfer out the fruit to the pineapple skins, decorate with the reserved pineapple leaves and serve.

COOK'S TIP

A ripe pineapple will resist pressure when squeezed and will have a sweet, fragrant smell. In winter, freezing conditions can cause the flesh to blacken.

Muscat Grape Frappé

The flavor and perfume of the Muscat grape is rarely more enticing than when captured in this sophisticated, icy-cool salad. Because of its alcohol content, this dish is not suitable for young children.

Serves 4

½ bottle Muscat wine, Beaumes de Venise, Frontignan or Rivesaltes

1 pound Muscat grapes

1 Pour the wine into a stainless-steel or enamel tray, add ⅔ cup water and freeze for 3 hours, or until the wine is completely solid.

2 Remove the seeds from the grapes with a pair of tweezers. If you have time, you can also peel the grapes. Scrape across the frozen wine with a tablespoon to make a fine ice. Combine the grapes with the ice, spoon into four shallow glasses and serve.

Grapefruit Salad with Campari and Orange

The bittersweet flavor of Campari combines especially well with citrus fruit such as grapefruit and oranges. Because of its alcohol content, this dish is not suitable for young children.

INGREDIENTS

Serves 4

3 tablespoons sugar

4 tablespoons Campari

2 tablespoons lemon juice

4 grapefruit

5 oranges

4 fresh mint sprigs, to decorate

1 Bring ⅔ cup water to a boil in a small saucepan, add the sugar and simmer until dissolved. Transfer to a bowl, let cool, then add the Campari and lemon juice. Chill until ready to serve.

2 Cut the peel from the top, bottom and sides of the grapefruit and oranges with a serrated knife. Segment the fruit into a bowl by slipping a small paring knife between the flesh and the membranes. Combine the fruit with the Campari syrup and chill.

3 Spoon the salad into four dishes, decorate with a sprig of fresh mint and serve.

COOK'S TIP

When buying citrus fruit, choose brightly-colored varieties that feel heavy for their size.

Dressed Strawberries

Fragrant strawberries release their finest flavor when moistened with a sauce of fresh raspberries and scented passionfruit.

INGREDIENTS

Serves 4

2 cups raspberries, fresh
   or frozen
3 tablespoons sugar
1 passionfruit
6 cups small strawberries
8 vanilla cookies, to serve

4 Pass the blended fruit sauce through a fine nylon sieve to remove the seeds.

5 Fold the strawberries into the sauce, then spoon into four stemmed glasses. Serve with vanilla cookies.

1 Place the raspberries and sugar in a stain-resistant saucepan and soften over low heat to release the juices. Simmer for 5 minutes. Let cool.

2 Halve the passionfruit and scoop out the seeds and juice.

3 Transfer the raspberries to a food processor or blender, add the passionfruit and blend until smooth.

Mixed Melon Salad with Wild Strawberries

Ice-cold melon is a delicious way to end a meal. Here several varieties are combined with strongly flavored wild or woodland strawberries. If wild berries are not available, use ordinary strawberries or raspberries.

INGREDIENTS

Serves 4

1 cantaloupe or Charentais melon

1 Galia melon

2 pounds watermelon

1½ cups wild strawberries

4 fresh mint sprigs, to decorate

1 Halve all the melons using a large knife.

2 Remove the seeds from the cantaloupe and galia melons with a spoon.

3 With a melon scoop, take out as many balls as you can from all three melons. Combine in a large bowl and refrigerate.

4 Add the wild strawberries and transfer to four stemmed glass dishes.

5 Decorate with sprigs of fresh mint and serve.

Fruit Kebabs with Mango and Yogurt Sauce

To enjoy these mixed fruit kebabs, dip them into the refreshingly minty mango and yogurt sauce.

INGREDIENTS

Serves 4

½ pineapple, peeled, cored and cubed

2 kiwi, peeled and cubed

scant 1 cup strawberries, hulled and cut in
    half lengthwise if large

½ mango, peeled, pitted and cubed

For the sauce

½ cup fresh mango purée, made from
    1–1½ peeled and pitted mangoes

½ cup plain yogurt

1 teaspoon sugar

few drops of vanilla extract

1 tablespoon finely shredded fresh
    mint leaves

1 fresh mint sprig, to decorate

1 To make the sauce, beat together the mango purée, yogurt, sugar and vanilla with an electric hand mixer.

2 Stir in the shredded mint. Cover the sauce and chill until needed.

3 Thread the fruit onto twelve 6-inch wooden skewers, alternating the pineapple, kiwi, strawberries and mango.

4 Transfer the mango and yogurt sauce to an attractive bowl, decorate with a mint sprig and place in the center of a large serving platter. Surround with the kebabs and serve.

Tropical Fruits in Cinnamon Syrup

These glistening fruits are best prepared a day in advance to let the flavors to develop and mingle.

INGREDIENTS

Serves 6

2¼ cups sugar

1 cinnamon stick

1 large or 2 medium papayas (about
    1½ pounds) peeled, seeded and cut
    lengthwise into thin pieces

1 large or 2 medium mangoes (about
    1½ pounds) peeled, pitted and cut
    lengthwise into thin pieces

1 large or 2 small star fruit (about
    8 ounces) thinly sliced

1 Sprinkle one third of the sugar on the bottom of a large saucepan. Add the cinnamon stick and half of the papaya, mango and star fruit pieces.

2 Sprinkle half of the remaining sugar on the fruit pieces in the pan. Add the remaining fruit and sprinkle with the remaining sugar.

3 Cover the pan and cook the fruit over medium heat for 35–45 minutes, until the sugar dissolves completely. Shake the pan occasionally, but do not stir or the fruit will collapse.

4 Uncover the pan and simmer for about 10 minutes, until the fruit begins to appear translucent. Remove the pan from the heat and let cool. Discard the cinnamon stick.

5 Transfer the fruit and syrup to a bowl, cover and refrigerate overnight before serving.

Banana and Mascarpone

If you are a fan of cold banana custard, you'll love this recipe. It is a grown-up version of an old favorite. No one will guess that the secret is ready-made custard sauce.

INGREDIENTS

Serves 4-6

generous 1 cup mascarpone cheese

1¼ cups fresh ready-made
    custard sauce

⅔ cup plain yogurt

4 bananas

juice of 1 lime

½ cup pecans,
    coarsely chopped

½ cup maple syrup

1 Combine the mascarpone, custard sauce and yogurt in a large bowl and beat until smooth. Make this mixture up to several hours ahead, if desired. Cover and chill, then stir before using.

2 Slice the bananas diagonally and place in a separate bowl. Pour on the lime juice and toss until the bananas are coated in the juice.

3 Divide half the custard mixture among four to six dessert glasses and top each portion with a generous spoonful of the banana mixture.

4 Spoon the remaining custard mixture into the glasses and top with the rest of the bananas. Sprinkle the nuts on top. Drizzle maple syrup onto each dessert and chill for 30 minutes before serving.

Bananas with Lime and Cardamom

Cardamom and bananas go together perfectly, and this luxurious dessert is an original treat.

INGREDIENTS

Serves 4

6 small bananas

¼ cup butter

seeds from 4 cardamom
    pods, crushed

½ cup sliced almonds

thinly pared zest and juice
    of 2 limes

⅓ cup light brown sugar

2 tablespoons dark rum

vanilla ice cream, to serve

1 Peel the bananas and cut them in half lengthwise. Heat half the butter in a large frying pan. Add half the bananas, and cook until the undersides are golden. Turn carefully, using a spatula. Cook until golden all over.

2 Once cooked, transfer the bananas to a heatproof serving dish. Cook the remaining bananas in the same way.

3 Melt the remaining butter, then add the cardamom seeds and almonds. Cook, stirring until the almonds are golden.

4 Stir in the lime zest and juice, then the sugar. Cook, stirring, until the mixture is smooth, bubbling and slightly reduced. Stir in the rum. Pour the sauce onto the bananas and serve immediately, with vanilla ice cream.

Melon Trio with Ginger Cookies

The eye-catching colors of these three different melons really make this dessert, while the crisp cookies provide a perfect contrast in terms of texture.

INGREDIENTS

Serves 4

¼ watermelon

½ honeydew melon

½ charentais melon

4 tablespoons stem ginger syrup

For the cookies

2 tablespoons unsalted butter

2 tablespoons sugar

1 teaspoon honey

¼ cup flour

¼ cup luxury candied
    mixed fruit, finely chopped

1 piece of stem ginger in syrup, drained
    and finely chopped

2 tablespoons sliced almonds

3 Line a baking sheet with non-stick baking paper. Space four spoonfuls of the mixture on the paper at regular intervals, leaving plenty of room for spreading. Flatten the mixture slightly into rounds and bake for 15 minutes or until the tops are golden.

4 Let the cookies cool on the baking sheet for 1 minute, then lift each one in turn, using a spatula, and drape over a rolling pin to cool and harden. Repeat with the remaining ginger mixture to make eight cookies in all.

5 Serve the melon chunks with some of the syrup and the ginger cookies.

COOK'S TIP

For an even prettier effect, scoop the melon flesh into balls with the large end of a melon baller.

1 Remove the seeds from the melons, cut them into wedges, then slice off the rind. Cut all the flesh into chunks and mix in a bowl. Stir in the ginger syrup, cover and chill until ready to serve.

2 Meanwhile, make the cookies. Preheat the oven to 350°F. Heat the butter, sugar and honey in a saucepan until melted. Remove from the heat and stir in the remaining ingredients.

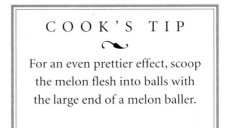

Jamaican Fruit Trifle

This trifle is actually based on a Caribbean fool that consists of fruit stirred into thick vanilla-flavored cream. This version is much less rich, redressing the balance with plenty of fruit and crème fraîche.

INGREDIENTS

Serves 8

1 large sweet pineapple, peeled and cored, about 12 ounces

1¼ cups heavy cream

scant 1 cup crème fraîche

4 tablespoons confectioners' sugar, sifted

2 teaspoons vanilla extract

2 tablespoons white or coconut rum

3 papayas, peeled, seeded and chopped

3 mangoes, peeled, pitted and chopped

thinly pared zest and juice of 1 lime

⅓ cup dry shredded coconut, toasted

1 Cut the pineapple into large chunks, place in a food processor or blender and process briefly until chopped. Transfer into a sieve placed over a bowl and let sit for 5 minutes so that most of the juice drains from the fruit.

2 Whip the heavy cream to very soft peaks, then lightly but thoroughly fold in the crème fraîche, sifted confectioners' sugar, vanilla extract and rum.

3 Fold the drained, chopped pineapple into the cream mixture. Place the chopped papayas and mangoes in a large bowl and pour on the lime juice. Gently stir the fruit mixture to combine. Shred the pared lime zest and add to the bowl.

4 Divide the fruit mixture and the pineapple cream among eight dessert plates. Decorate with the lime shreds, toasted coconut and a few small pineapple leaves, if desired, and serve immediately.

COOK'S TIP

It is important to let the pineapple purée drain thoroughly, otherwise, the pineapple cream will be watery. Don't throw away the drained pineapple juice—mix it with mineral water for a refreshing drink.

Tropical Fruit Gratin

This out-of-the-ordinary gratin is strictly for grown-ups. A colorful combination of fruit is topped with a simple sabayon before being browned under the broiler.

INGREDIENTS

Serves 4

2 tamarillos

½ sweet pineapple

1 ripe mango

1½ cups blackberries

½ cup sparkling white wine

½ cup sugar

6 egg yolks

1 Cut each tamarillo in half lengthwise and then into thick slices. Cut the rind and core from the pineapple and take spiral slices off the outside to remove the eyes. Cut the flesh into chunks. Peel the mango, cut it in half and cut the flesh from the pit in slices.

2 Divide all the fruit, including the blackberries, among four 5½-inch gratin dishes set on a baking sheet and set aside. Heat the wine and sugar in a saucepan until the sugar has dissolved. Bring to a boil, and cook for 5 minutes.

3 Put the egg yolks in a large heatproof bowl. Place the bowl over a pan of simmering water and whisk until pale. Slowly pour on the hot sugar syrup, whisking constantly, until the mixture thickens. Preheat the broiler.

4 Spoon the mixture onto the fruit. Place the baking sheet holding the dishes on a low shelf under the hot broiler until the topping is golden. Serve hot.

Grilled Pineapple with Papaya Sauce

Pineapple cooked this way takes on a superb flavor and is sensational when served with the papaya sauce.

INGREDIENTS

Serves 6

1 sweet pineapple

melted butter, for greasing and brushing

2 pieces drained stem ginger in
   syrup, cut into fine matchsticks, plus
    2 tablespoons of the syrup from the jar

2 tablespoons brown sugar

pinch of ground cinnamon

fresh mint sprigs, to decorate

For the sauce

1 ripe papaya, peeled and seeded

¾ cup apple juice

1 Peel the pineapple and take spiral slices off the outside to remove the eyes. Cut it crosswise into six slices, each 1-inch thick. Line a baking sheet with a sheet of foil, rolling up the sides to make a rim. Grease the foil with melted butter. Preheat the broiler.

2 Arrange the pineapple slices on the lined baking sheet. Brush with butter, then top with the ginger matchsticks, sugar and cinnamon. Drizzle on the stem ginger syrup. Broil for 5–7 minutes or until the slices are golden and lightly charred on top.

3 Meanwhile, make the sauce. Cut a few slices from the papaya and set aside, then purée the rest with the apple juice in a blender or food processor.

4 Press the purée through a sieve placed over a bowl, then stir in any juices from cooking the pineapple. Serve the pineapple slices with a little sauce drizzled around each plate. Decorate with the reserved papaya slices and the mint sprigs.

Citrus Fruit Flambé

A fruit flambé makes a dramatic finale for a dinner party. Topping this refreshing citrus fruit dessert with crunchy pistachio praline makes it extra special.

INGREDIENTS

Serves 4

4 oranges

2 ruby grapefruit

2 limes

¼ cup butter

⅓ cup light brown sugar

3 tablespoons Cointreau

fresh mint sprigs, to decorate

For the praline

oil, for greasing

½ cup sugar

½ cup pistachios, shelled

1 First, make the pistachio praline. Brush a baking sheet lightly with oil. Place the sugar and nuts in a small heavy saucepan and cook gently, swirling the pan occasionally, until the sugar has melted.

2 Continue to cook over fairly low heat until the nuts start to pop and the sugar has turned a dark golden color. Pour onto the oiled baking sheet and set aside to cool. Using a sharp knife, chop the praline into rough chunks.

3 Cut all the zest and pith from the citrus fruits. Holding each fruit in turn over a large bowl, cut between the membranes so that the segments fall into the bowl, with any juice.

4 Heat the butter and brown sugar together in a heavy frying pan until the sugar has melted and the mixture is golden. Strain the citrus juices into the pan and continue to cook, stirring occasionally, until the juice has reduced and is syrupy.

5 Add the fruit segments and warm through without stirring. Pour on the Cointreau and set it alight. As soon as the flames die down, spoon the fruit flambé into serving dishes. Sprinkle some praline on each portion and decorate with mint.

Exotic Fruit Salad

Passion fruit makes a superb dressing for any fruit, but really brings out the flavor of exotic varieties. You can easily double the recipe, then serve the rest for the next day's breakfast.

Serves 6

1 mango

1 papaya

2 kiwi fruits

coconut or vanilla ice cream, to serve

For the dressing

3 passionfruit

thinly pared zest and juice of 1 lime

1 teaspoon hazelnut or walnut oil

1 tablespoon honey

1 Peel the mango, cut it into three slices, then cut the flesh into chunks and place it in a large bowl. Peel the papaya and cut it in half. Scoop out the seeds, then chop the flesh.

2 Cut both ends off each kiwi, then stand them on a board. Using a small sharp knife, cut off the skin from top to bottom. Cut each kiwi in half lengthwise, then cut into thick slices. Combine all the fruit in a large bowl.

3 Make the dressing. Cut each passion fruit in half and scoop the seeds out into a sieve set over a small bowl. Press the seeds well to extract all their juices. Lightly whisk the remaining dressing ingredients into the passion fruit juice, then pour the dressing onto the fruit. Mix gently. Let chill for 1 hour before serving with scoops of coconut or vanilla ice cream.

COOK'S TIP

A clear golden honey scented with orange blossom or acacia blossom would be perfect for the dressing.

Index